GORE VIDAL

MODERN LITERATURE SERIES

GENERAL EDITOR: Philip Winsor

In the same series:

(*continued on last page of book*)

GORE VIDAL

Robert F. Kiernan

FREDERICK UNGAR PUBLISHING CO.
NEW YORK

Library of Congress Cataloging in Publication Data

Kiernan, Robert F.
  Gore Vidal.

  (Modern literature series)
  Bibliography: p.
  Includes index.
  1. Vidal, Gore, 1925–   —Criticism and
interpretation. I. Title. II. Series.
PS3543.I26Z75   818′ .5409   81–70962
ISBN 0–8044–2461–6   AACR2
ISBN 0–8044–6360–3 (pbk.)

iv

In memory of Beatrice Velten Kiernan

Contents

Chronology

1 The Life   1

2 The Vidalian Manner: *The Judgment of Paris, Two Sisters, Kalki*   10

3 The Early Successes: *Williwaw, The City and the Pillar*   32

4 The Ancient World: *Julian, Creation*   45

5 The American Trilogy: *Washington, D.C., Burr, 1876*   67

6 The Breckinridge Novels   94

7 The Essays   110

8 The Minor Works   118

9 A Summary Assessment   142

Notes   145

Bibliography   153

Index   157

Acknowledgments

I have several times threatened that in lieu of the usual prefatory rhetoric ("faults entirely my own," and so forth) I would announce in this space that all inaccuracies and infelicities must be credited to those who read the material in draft form. Else what's a reader for? It is a pleasure, instead, to thank my readers for their assistance. I am deeply indebted to Manhattan College Professors Mary Ann O'Donnell and John Nagle, dear friends both, who read the full text and suggested many improvements. I am indebted also to Professor Ernest Speranza, my favorite linguist, for clarifying several points of usage. Once again I must acknowledge the kindnesses of Máire Duchon of the Cardinal Hayes Library, Manhattan College; the courtesies also of librarians at the New York City Public Library, the Beinecke and Sterling Libraries at Yale University, and the Wisconsin Historical Society.

Chronology

1925   Eugene Luther Vidal born to Eugene and Nina Gore Vidal on October 3 at the United States Military Academy, West Point, New York. Family moves shortly thereafter to Washington, D.C.; lives with his maternal grandfather, Senator Thomas Pryor Gore of Oklahoma.

1935   Parents divorced; mother marries Hugh D. Auchincloss. Attends St. Alban's School in Washington. Lives at Merrywood, the Auchincloss estate in Virginia.

1939   Graduates from St. Alban's. Tours England and Europe during the summer and studies briefly at Château du Mont Cel, Seine-et-disè, France, as part of tour. Enters Los Alamos School, Los Alamos, New Mexico, in September. Renames himself Gore Vidal while at school.

1940   Leaves Los Alamos School in June and enrolls in September at Phillips Exeter Academy, Exeter, New Hampshire.

1941   Mother divorces Hugh D. Auchincloss.

1943   Graduates from Phillips Exeter Academy. Joins U.S. Army 30 July; sent to Virginia Military Institute for one term to study engineering.

1944   Appointed to rank of Maritime Warrant Officer and assigned to Peterson Field,

Colorado, effective October 24. Begins writing *Williwaw*.

1945   Appointed First Mate of *F.S. 35*, Army Transport Service in the Aleutian Islands, effective January 29. Hospitalized in Los Angeles for arthritis; transferred to Florida. Meets Anaïs Nin. Completes *Williwaw*.

1946   Transferred to Mitchell Field, New York; discharged from Army February 15. Works six months as editor for New York publishing firm of E. P. Dutton. *Williwaw* published.

1947   Maintains primary residence in Antigua, Guatemala, through 1949. Writes *The Season of Comfort*. *In a Yellow Wood* published.

1948   *The City and the Pillar* published. Tours Europe in spring and winter; meets Paul Bowles, Christopher Isherwood, André Gide, and George Santayana en route. Motors in Italy with Tennessee Williams.

1949   Completes *Dark Green, Bright Red* in Antigua. Winters in New Orleans and writes short stories. Senator Gore dies. *The Season of Comfort* published.

1950   Purchases house at Barrytown-on-Hudson, New York. Lectures widely. Begins *The Judgment of Paris*. *A Search for the King* and *Dark Green, Bright Red* published.

1951   Lectures widely. Completes *The Judgment of Paris*. Begins to live with Howard Austen.

1952   *The Judgment of Paris* published. *Death in the Fifth Position* published under pseudonym Edgar Box.

1953   Lectures widely. *Death Before Bedtime* published under pseudonym Edgar Box.

1954   Begins two years of writing and adapting for television. "Dark Possession" televised February 15; "Smoke," May 4; "Barn Burning,"

August 17; others. *Messiah* published. *Death Likes It Hot* published under pseudonym Edgar Box.

1955   Continues to write and adapt for television. "A Sense of Justice" televised February 6; "The Turn of the Screw," February 13; "Stage Door," May 8; "A Farewell to Arms," May 26; "The Death of Billy the Kid," July 24; "Dr. Jekyll and Mr. Hyde," July 28; others. Receives Edgar Allan Poe award for television drama. Visits California to investigate possibility of writing film scripts.

1956   Tours Europe in the spring. Signs four-year contract with MGM. Visits London to write script for film *I Accuse.* Film *The Catered Affair* (screenplay by Vidal) released. "Portrait of a Ballerina" televised January 1; "Honor," June 19; others. *A Thirsty Evil* and *Visit to a Small Planet and Other Television Plays* published.

1957   Purchases New York City town house as *pied-à-terre. Visit to a Small Planet* opens on Broadway February 7 and runs for 338 performances. Productions also in Wilmington, Delaware, and San Francisco. *Visit to a Small Planet* published.

1958   Visits London to write script for film *The Scapegoat.* Films *I Accuse* (screenplay by Vidal) and *The Left-Handed Gun* (screenplay allegedly by Vidal) released.

1959   Writes drama reviews for *The Reporter;* begins writing *Julian.* Films *Ben Hur* (some dialogue by Vidal), *The Scapegoat* (adaptation by Vidal), and *Suddenly, Last Summer* (screenplay by Vidal) released. Writes and narrates "The Indestructible Mr. Gore," televised December 13.

1960   *The Best Man* opens on Broadway March 31
        and runs for 520 performances. Runs for Con-
        gress in Twenty-ninth District of New York;
        defeated. *On the March to the Sea* produced
        in Hyde Park, New York. "Dear Arthur" tele-
        vised March 22. *The Best Man* published.

1961   Writes political commentaries for *Esquire*
        and theater pieces for *Partisan Review. On
        the March to the Sea* produced in Germany.

1962   *Romulus* opens on Broadway January 10 and
        runs for 69 performances. *Rocking the Boat,
        Three,* and *Three Plays* are published.

1963   Tours southern Europe and Near East. Lives
        in Rome much of the year, completing *Julian*
        and revising *The City and the Pillar.* Begins
        writing frequently for *New York Review of
        Books.*

1964   Rejects second chance to run for Congress.
        Julian published. Hosts *Hot Line* television
        interview program October through Decem-
        ber. Film *The Best Man* (screenplay by Vidal)
        released.

1965   Lives in Europe and collaborates on film
        scripts of *Is Paris Burning?* and *The Night of
        the Generals.* Revised versions of *The City
        and the Pillar, The Judgment of Paris,* and
        Messiah published.

1966   Lives in Paris and Rome, finishing *Washing-
        ton, D.C. Romulus* published.

1967   Sells house in Barrytown-on-Hudson; settles
        in Rome and maintains primary residence in
        Italy through the 1970s, with extended so-
        journs in the United States, Switzerland, and
        Ireland. *Washington, D.C.* published.

1968   *Weekend* opens on Broadway March 13 and
        runs for 22 performances. Campaigns for
        Senator Eugene McCarthy. Infamous televi-

sion exchange with William F. Buckley, Jr., at the Republican convention at Miami Beach. Co-founds "New Party" at the Democratic convention at Chicago. Revised version of *Dark Green, Bright Red* published. *Myra Breckinridge* and *Sex, Death and Money* published.

1969 Father dies. *Reflections Upon a Sinking Ship* published.

1970 *A Drawing Room Comedy* produced outside New York City. Becomes co-chairman of "People's Party" (which absorbs "New Party") for two years. Film *The Last of the Mobile Hot Shots* (screenplay by Vidal) released. *Two Sisters* published.

1972 *Homage to Daniel Shays: Collected Essays 1952–1972* published. *An Evening with Richard Nixon and . . .* opens on Broadway April 30 and runs for 17 performances and 13 revised performances. *An Evening with Richard Nixon* published. Purchases villa in Ravello, Italy.

1973 *Burr* published.

1974 *Myron* published.

1976 *1876* published. Establishes primary residence in Los Angeles to escape new Italian tax laws.

1977 *Matters of Fact and of Fiction (Essays 1973–1976)* published. Begins habit of summering in Italy, wintering in California.

1978 *Kalki* published. Works on screenplay for *Gore Vidal's Caligula* but withdraws from project, and name is removed from title of completed film. Omnibus volume *Gore Vidal* published.

1980 Sells New York City town house; buys house in Hollywood Hills, California. Works on screenplays for *Dress Gray* (rejected), *Kalki*, and film about Huey Long.

1981 *Creation* published. Announces possible candidacy for the Senate in 1982.

1
The Life

Gore Vidal has chosen to wear several different public manners. There is the patrician manner, for instance, cool, elegant, and somewhat haughty, that belongs to Vidal the guest of television interviewers. There is the outré manner, witty, risqué, and obstreperous, that belongs to Vidal the impulsive camp. And there is the intellectual manner, epigrammatic, iconoclastic, and cheerless, that belongs to Vidal the political commentator. These manners and others that are shadings or combinations of them are carried off with aplomb by Vidal both in his life and in his writings; but they are indubitably *manners*, stylizations of the self that conceal as much of the man as they reveal. By all accounts, Vidal is a very private person at the same time that he is a self-confessed exhibitionist. His way of reconciling these divergent impulses is to forge out of elements in his character an assortment of exaggerated public selves that perplex us in their array, keeping us distant but also keeping us watchful.

Vidal's affectation of patrician hauteur is not without basis. His American roots can be traced on his mother's side to the seventeenth century, and his maternal grandfather was the blind statesman Thomas Pryor Gore (1870–1949), Oklahoma's first

United States senator. Although Vidal was born in the Cadet Hospital at West Point, where his father was completing an appointment as an instructor, Vidal lived with his parents until he was ten years old in Senator Gore's mansion in the District of Columbia, where he grew accustomed to life among the notable. Vidal's mother, Nina Gore, enjoyed the role of a Washington socialite in her father's home. After her divorce from Vidal's father and her marriage to Hugh D. Auchincloss, both in 1935, Vidal lived at the Auchincloss estate on the Potomac River, where he continued to mingle casually with the socially prominent. "It was a world of the rich and the powerful," Vidal has said, "who were able to keep unpleasant things far from them."[1] After completing primary studies at St. Alban's School in 1939, Vidal followed the classic pattern of privileged youth: a quick tour of Europe before the advent of World War II, one year at the Los Alamos School in New Mexico, and then three years at Phillips Exeter Academy in New Hampshire, where his acquaintances were once again from among the socially elite.

Vidal's father, Eugene Luther Vidal, could trace his family to sixteenth-century Italy, but the Vidals did not arrive in America until 1848, and Nina Gore apparently came to think the Vidals déclassé and her husband a social disadvantage. Yet Vidal's father seems to have been an intelligent and decent man, successful in the American mode. He was a football hero at West Point, a competitor in the 1920 Olympics, and an instructor in aeronautics at West Point until shortly after his son's birth. He served President Roosevelt as Director of Air Commerce from 1933 to 1937, and after his divorce he founded a successful aircraft company. Vidal remembers his father with considerably more affection than his mother, yet at the age of fourteen he abandoned his patronymic birth name in favor of the metronymic Gore Vidal, delighting, no doubt, in the name's patrician ring.

We have only scattered glimpses of the young Gore Vidal. In the autobiographical short story "A Moment of Green Laurel," Vidal meets his half-grown self outside his grandfather's stone house in Rock Creek Park, and he depicts himself as a quietly outspoken child given free rein in his grandfather's attic library. Other biographical evidence[2] authenticates Vidal's depiction of himself in the story, and one guesses that Senator Gore was young Vidal's role model, for at fourteen Vidal attended his first presidential convention, and at Exeter he was a dedicated Anglophobe, an isolationist, and an America Firster in imitation of his grandfather's idiosyncratic populism. Two years Vidal's junior at Exeter, the novelist John Knowles used Vidal as the model for Brinker Hadley, the adolescent politician of *A Separate Peace* (1959), and we glimpse something of Vidal's brittle precocity at Exeter in the caricature.

The diarist Anaïs Nin, briefly Vidal's confidante, wrote of him in her 1944–47 diary, "He has something of the frozen adolescent who has not yet melted with trust, passion. He is tight." She also affords us a glimpse of Vidal's relationship with his mother: "Psychologically he knows the meaning of his mother abandoning him when he was ten, to remarry and have other children," she wrote, and in another entry she observed dispassionately, "He had wanted his mother to die."[3] Vidal's graduation yearbook from Exeter offers a particularly devastating glimpse into his adolescent posturing, listing him as "Class Hypocrite." The composite portrait suggests that Vidal learned to stylize himself at an early age and to protect his youthful ego under a mannered sophistication.

In 1943, two months after completing his formal

schooling at Phillips Exeter, Vidal enlisted in the
Army Reserve Corps; after a series of clerical jobs, he
became first mate on an Army transport ship in the
Aleutian Islands. Vidal's first novel, *Williwaw*, was
begun aboard that ship and was based upon his maritime experience, but the novel was completed in
California and Florida while Vidal recuperated from
rheumatoid arthritis that developed in the Alaskan
climate, and the powerful storm scene in the novel
was actually based on a Florida hurricane, not on the
Arctic storm called by Indians a "williwaw." *Williwaw* was Vidal's fourth attempt to write a novel,
and its completion gave him the confidence to write
In a Yellow Wood while he was stationed at Mitchell
Field in New York and supposedly writing a history
of the base. Neither *Williwaw* nor *In a Yellow Wood*
was published, however, until Vidal was discharged
from the Army and employed as an editor by the
publishing firm of E. P. Dutton. Dutton published
Williwaw in 1946 to favorable reviews, and Vidal
resigned his position in the firm immediately; he is
proud that he has not worked in an office since then.
Dutton published *In a Yellow Wood* in 1947, also to
favorable reviews.

But it was *The City and the Pillar* (1948) that
brought Vidal notoriety, for he coolly represented an
all-American boy as a homosexual in that novel. *The
City and the Pillar* is not sexually graphic, but it
distinguishes several homosexual types and so
seemed to many to be wallowing in filth. *The New
York Times* refused to accept advertising for the
book, and the critics gave Vidal's next five novels
minimal notice in what appears to have been a deliberate snub. It was not Vidal's first employment of
homosexual material. He had begun a novel about
homosexuality as early as 1943, when he was still a
student at Exeter,[4] and he had drawn a homosexual

character in *In a Yellow Wood*. But it was the first time that his homosexual motif had been found sensational. Vidal was very proud of *The City and the Pillar* and its considerable sales, and he was heartened by the support of Paul Bowles, Christopher Isherwood, Tennessee Williams, André Gide, and George Santayana, all of whom were introduced to him in Europe early in 1948, just after the novel's publication. Gide even presented him with a copy of *Corydon* (1924) inscribed "as one prophet to another." Tennessee Williams became his particularly close friend, and together they jaunted through Italy in the madcap fashion that was to become the style of their friendship.

Except for periods of vacationing in the United States and Europe, Vidal lived inexpensively in Guatemala after his resignation from Dutton, supporting himself on royalties from *The City and the Pillar*. But the commercial failure of *The Season of Comfort* (1949), *Dark Green, Bright Red* (1950), *A Search for the King* (1950), *The Judgment of Paris* (1952), and *Messiah* (1954) finally rendered his financial position acute, especially after he spent $16,000 of borrowed money in 1950 to purchase a house called Edgewater in Barrytown-on-Hudson, New York. Vidal had a small income from his father, but the 1820 mansion was expensive to maintain, and Vidal found it necessary to abandon the novel for more lucrative forms of writing.

As soon as he was settled in Edgewater, Vidal proceeded to write several detective novels which he published under the coy pseudonym Edgar Box, but *Death in the Fifth Position* (1952), *Death Before Bedtime* (1953), and *Death Likes It Hot* (1954) enjoyed only modest success. Encouraged by his literary agent, Vidal turned to screenplays, for American television was just entering its so-called Golden Age and devouring screenplays omnivorously. Ultimately, Vidal wrote nearly a hundred scripts for programs such as *Suspense, Omnibus,* and *Studio One.* He found scripting to his taste, despite considering it hack work, and he produced a number of scripts comparable to those of Paddy Chayefsky and Rod Serling. Among these are "Visit to a Small Planet" (televised May 8, 1955), "The Death of Billy the Kid" (July 24, 1955), and adaptations of William Faulkner's "Barn Burning" (August 17, 1954) and Henry James's *The Turn of the Screw* (February 13, 1955). A testimonial to Senator Gore that Vidal wrote and narrated for *Sunday Showcase* (December 13, 1959) is of especial interest.

When the television market for live drama ebbed in the late 1950s, Vidal turned to Hollywood and Broadway. Under a four-year contract with MGM, he wrote the scenarios of *The Catered Affair* (1956), *I Accuse* (1958), *The Scapegoat* (1959),[5] and *Suddenly, Last Summer* (1959), and he was one of several collaborators on the scenario of *Ben Hur* (1959). Later he was to contribute to the scenarios of *Is Paris Burning?* (1966) and *The Night of the Generals* (1967), although he did not receive screen credit for either. Vidal's interest in the legitimate theater has always been small compared to his interest in film, but during the MGM period he expanded "Visit to a Small Planet" into a Broadway play which opened on February 7, 1957, with Cyril Ritchard in the lead, and which played for 338 performances. In the wake of that success, he wrote a political melodrama entitled *The Best Man.* The play opened on March 31, 1969, with Frank Lovejoy and Melvyn Douglas in the cast and ran for an impressive 520 performances. *Romulus* (1962), adapted from Friedrich Dürrenmatt's *Romulus der Grosse,* was unsuccessful, however, as was *An Evening with Richard Nixon and . . .* (1972) a decade later.

Vidal has described the 1950s as the period of his "head-on encounter with the world."[6] The encounter reached its climax in 1960 when Vidal ran for Congress as a Democrat-Liberal in New York's traditionally Republican Twenty-ninth District. His advocacy of recognizing mainland China, decreasing the national defense budget, and increasing federal aid to education predictably caused him to lose the election, even though he was endorsed by his friends Eleanor Roosevelt, Joanne Woodward, and Paul Newman. He lost to an entrenched candidate by a smaller margin than anyone had anticipated, however, and what was thought to have been a cavalier bid for office seemed a reasonable aspiration after the vote was in.

Defeat at the polls did not dissuade Vidal from further political advocacy. In 1961 he wrote a series of political columns for *Esquire*, and in the years since then he has published a number of iconoclastic political essays in *The New York Review of Books* and *The New Statesman*. An accomplished conversationalist, Vidal has also been a frequent guest on television talk shows since the early 1960s, and his conversational theme has generally been politics. His most noted television moment occurred in a debate with William F. Buckley, Jr., during the 1968 Republican convention. Vidal several times called Buckley a "pro-crypto-Nazi," and Buckley finally retorted, "Now listen, you queer. Stop calling me a crypto-Nazi or I'll sock you in your goddamn face." Fisticuffs did not ensue, but lawsuits did, and the episode is emblazoned on the public mind as a testament to high style run amok.[7]

His finances secure and his bid for public office behind him, Vidal adopted a newly relaxed mode of

life in the early 1960s, settling quietly in Italy with
Howard Austen, his companion since 1951, and re-
turning after a hiatus of ten years to the writing of
novels. *Julian* (1964) is not only the first of Vidal's
novels written in Italy, it is also the first novel of his
artistic maturity, for the imitative and flat voice of
the early fiction is counterpointed in *Julian* by several voices recognizably Vidal's own, full of bitchy vitality and conversational élan. *Julian* quickly reached
the best-seller lists, and its success inspired Vidal to
publish revised versions of *The City and the Pillar,
The Judgment of Paris,* and *Messiah* in 1965. Since
then, Vidal has published a new novel almost every
two years, with the subjects of the novels closely
linked to his interests. *Washington, D.C.* (1967), *Burr*
(1973), and *1876* (1976) reflect his abiding interest in
American government; *Myra Breckinridge* (1968)
and *Myron* (1974) reflect his encyclopedic knowledge of films; and *Two Sisters* (1970), *Kalki* (1978),
and *Creation* (1981) reflect his deep-seated interests
in the ancient world, in religious pretension, and in
the apocalyptic moment.

Vidal has always maintained American citizen-
ship and paid American taxes, but for most of the
1960s and 1970s he regarded the apartment in Rome
and the villa in Ravello as his homes, and it is in those
places that he has written most of the novels since
Julian. During those decades he spent months at a
time away from Italy, however, favoring at different
periods Switzerland, Ireland, New York, and California. New Italian tax laws in 1976 necessitated that
Vidal spend less than six months of every year in
Italy, and so he purchased a home in Los Angeles and
now divides his time between California and Italy.
Confessing to occasional boredom with the "sullen,
solitary joys of prose,"[8] he has also begun to interest
himself professionally in films once again. His screen-

play for a projected film *Gore Vidal's Caligula* fell
victim to a vulgar elaboration by the director Tinto
Brass, however; at Vidal's insistence, his name was
excised from the finished *Caligula* (1980).

"Gore Vidal wasn't what I set out to be," Vidal
once quipped. "But I don't mind what I've
become."[9] But just as Vidal's affected langour conceals disciplined work habits and careful scholarship,
one suspects that his self-assurance conceals a profound sense of failure, for his fiction has not received
the serious respect that Vidal wants. Indeed, one suspects a degree of bluster in Vidal's rigorous and re-
peated insistence that he is the most fortunate of
writers. But Vidal is a very private person, and the
public selves he crafts are entertaining, vital, and
stylish. If the uncrafted self remains his secret, what
loss to us?

2
The Vidalian Manner:
The Judgment of Paris,
Two Sisters, Kalki

Vidal is a difficult writer to categorize because he is a man of several voices. He has brooded over ancient empires in several novels, as though he were possessed by the spirit of Gibbon, yet he has also written about the American *crise de virilité* and managed to sound a good deal like Hemingway. He has sent young Americans in search of Old Europe, as a dutiful son of Henry James, but he has also written novels about the American political system and acknowledged a debt to Henry Adams. In his essays he often seems like Lord Macaulay, magisterial and urbane, while in the Breckinridge novels he evokes Ronald Firbank, irrepressible and playful.

Nevertheless, there are aspects of Vidal's writing that are constant. Syntactically elegant sentences are a trademark, certainly, and understated structures and a coolness of tone are too. More than anything else, however, we have learned to expect amplitude from Vidal. We have learned to expect that his narratives will be enriched with gossip, incidental satire, self-mockery, and philosophical and historical asides, very much in the eighteenth-century mode of Laurence Sterne and other giants of the early English novel. Concomitantly, we have learned to expect antique literary forms from Vidal, as if they were necessary to accommodate this old-world amplitude. Thus, his writings include historical fiction, moral essays, nonsense tales, mythography, and apocalyptic parables.

But Vidal is as much prankster as pundit, and his elegance, coolness, and learning derive a special piquancy from a wit always at the ready. "I am at heart a propagandist," he has written of himself, "a tremendous hater, a tiresome nag, complacently positive that there is no human problem which could not be solved if people would simply do as I advise."[1] There, in a sentence, is the Vidalian manner: the arrogance of the pundit solemnly and unabashedly put forth but undercut and put in amenable focus by the prankster's wit.

The Judgment of Paris (1952, revised 1965) is in several ways typical of Vidal's novels. Its central character is Philip Warren, a twenty-eight-year-old American just graduated from Harvard Law School, who dallies in Europe for a year with the intention of deciding at leisure what to do with the rest of his life. Three women dominate this *Wanderjahr*, and each suggests a different mode of life that Philip might pursue. He meets the first woman, Regina Durham, in Rome. She is a behind-the-scenes power in American politics, and she offers to create a major political career for Warren, not merely because she enjoys his bed but because she would enjoy managing his life. He meets the second woman, Sophia Oliver, in Egypt. An archeologist, she advises Warren to undertake a dispassionate intellectual life, reasoning that ideas are more real and more lasting than the thinkers who conceive them. The third woman, Anna Morris, Warren follows to Paris after an encounter in Cairo. She is the wife of an American businessman, and she offers Warren occasional in-

timacies and love. At the end of the novel Warren
rejects both Regina's public life and Sophia's intellectual life in favor of Anna's offerings, even though he
knows that she will never leave her husband and that
he may never see her again.

As the title of the novel suggests, its tripartite
plot is based loosely on the incident in Greek mythology in which Hermes brings the goddesses Hera,
Athena, and Aphrodite to Paris so that he may judge
which is the most beautiful. Hera, the wife of Zeus,
offers Paris kingship in return for his vote, and
Athena, the goddess of war, offers him skill in battle
(Vidal chooses to emphasize Athena's equally important role as the goddess of wisdom). It is of course
Aphrodite, the goddess of love, whom Paris chooses,
just as Philip finally chooses Anna's love.

It is entirely typical of Vidal that he treats this
important aspect of his novel unimportantly and
more or less ignores its ideational structure. Indeed,
Warren chooses only superficially among the power,
knowledge, and love that his three women dangle
before him, for Regina's life of power and Sophia's
life of knowledge hold no allure for him, and he has
no illusion that the world would be well lost for Anna's will-o'-the-wisp love. What Warren really
chooses—almost consciously—is to step out of himself for the first time in his life and to connect vitally
with another human being. Having a considerable
fear of death, a marked distaste for physical contact,
and some reluctance even to be understood, he
senses accurately that he holds his selfhood too tightly and that his future should involve more than the
self-aggrandizement that Regina and Sophia would
foster. As he turns to Anna in the last paragraph of
the novel, it is significant that a mirror dissolves mys-
tically before his eyes, "dispelling its ungrieved
ghosts like smoke upon the night," and that he passes

beyond that narcissistic mirror into a "promise at the present's furthest edge."

At the climax of his *Wanderjahr*, then, Warren chooses between two kinds of psychic orientation, not among the more obvious choices arrayed in the mythic analogue. Since the myth coincides with Warren's psyche so imperfectly, one even wonders whether Vidal means to disparage the modernist belief that mythology provides a gloss for every psychological state. I think it more likely that Vidal is simply not very interested in his plot, especially since Warren's decision to relax his hold on selfhood has little dramatic substance and is scarcely more successful than the myth in holding the novel together. Vidal typically understates his plots, in fact, as if plotting were alien to his auctorial sensibility. When he does not under*state* the plots, he is apt to under*mine* them, parodying the need for plot.

Vidal understates his main characters, too. Philip Warren is a rather dim young man, not exactly naïve but amenable to the point of vacuity. Regina Durham is a decently rounded character, but Sophia Oliver never engages the reader's interest, and Anna Morris is hardly characterized at all. On the basis of such understatement, the critic John W. Aldridge has likened *The Judgment of Paris* and the novels that precede it to badly balanced darts thrown at a moving target. "They have never been entirely successful because they have never known precisely where they were supposed to go," Aldridge wrote in 1952, voicing an opinion of Vidal's novels still current today. "Too many of them appear to have been written not out of a deep urge in Vidal to get something said, but out of a disturbing suspicion that, having missed the target the first time, he had better throw another dart."[2]

The metaphor is shrewd, but I find Aldridge un-

duly puristic in censuring the early novels simply
because Vidal has no overriding passion to vent, no
overriding vision to impart. A less solemn notion of
the writer's obligation would suggest that Vidal
treats his typical story line rather like a clothesline,
hanging on the story line whatever turns up in his
literary hamper. There is an abundance of both
minor plots and minor characters in *The Judgment of
Paris,* certainly, none of which has much to do with
the novel's larger plot and all of which hang rather
shapelessly on the line—but each is in itself a marvelous bit of color, an *objet trouvé,* as it were.

In the first section of the novel, Warren becomes
entangled with the homosexual dilettantes Clyde
Norman and Lord Ayre Glenellen and their mad plot
to restore the Italian monarchy. Acting as Glenellen's
reluctant courier, Warren tries to deliver a message
to the eccentric Signor Guiscardo, who affects animal
masks as a disguise. Warren makes an appointment
to deliver his message in the ruins of a mountain
chapel at midnight, but Guiscardo fails to keep this
Gothic assignation, and an animal mask abandoned
in the ruins is the only clue that some mysterious fate
has befallen him. The message entrusted to Warren
is melodramatically cryptic: it is the single Greek
word *asebia,* which connotes a failure to worship the
gods. Glenellen subsequently denies having sent the
message, of course, and in a dazzling turnabout aban-
dons his campaign to restore the house of Savoy and
becomes, illogically, a communist. He surfaces again
in the third section of the novel as part of a ludicrous
transvestite cult that revolves around an androgyne
known alternately as Augusta and Augustus.

The flip-flop inconsequence of all this is not without point. The string of incidents is both a parody of
spy fiction and a camp trivialization of homosexualist
interests, and it is ultimately an attack on the literary

mystique of plot, inasmuch as the Norman-Glenellen axis of events succeeds as a kind of plot despite its alogical seriality.

Each of the two later sections of the novel has a string of events that similarly defies the mystique of plot. The Egypt section introduces a man named Briggs Willys who is afflicted with *taedium vitae* but cannot manage to organize a suicide despite several sincere attempts. He therefore engages Mrs. Fay Peabody, a doyenne of detective fiction, to dispatch his very considerable flesh. Regarding the assignment as a challenge to her plotting ability (she is Agatha Christie, thinly disguised), Mrs. Peabody sets in motion a series of harebrained murder schemes that evoke the airier flights of the locked-room detection novel. All of them, of course, fail dismally. The Paris section of the novel deals not only with the cult of the androgyne, in which Glenellen's plotting instinct finds an outlet in a pseudo-religious vesting ritual, but also with the plots of a stupendously vulgar hostess named Zoe Helotius to crash the royal house of Windsor. Mrs. Helotius is as mad in her own way as Mrs. Peabody, Lord Glenellen, and Signor Guiscardo, and such highly colored characters throw Warren's bland sanity into nice relief, just as their madcap plots flatter the understatement of the novel's main plot.

Indeed, this understatement of the main plot allows Vidal to expend a wealth of invention on minor characters without creating an aesthetic imbalance. The octogenarian Duchesse de Lyon et Grenoble, who grandly mishears everything that is said to her; a Russian spy who pretends to be an Indian princess and speaks of herself in the third person under the impression that she is using the royal plural; a field marshal who tears apart prize roses, *pace* Dickens: all are bits of color in the novel's

bright motley. Vidal's understated plot also allows
him to adorn the novel with a wealth of interesting
asides, such as Warren's speculation that energetic
mediocrity is politically more useful in a republican
society than brilliance, wit, or passion, and Mr. Norman's speculation that Europe's old-world manners
would have expired long since had it not been for the
unexpected applause of the Western cousins.

Even more important, perhaps, the understatement of the basic story line allows relatively free rein
to Vidal's wit. He has a great deal of fun with homosexuality and spoofs the reputation as homosexual
novelist that *The City and the Pillar* had earned him.
His joke is that Philip Warren is relentlessly *hetero-*
sexual, although homosexuals dominate the circles
he moves in. Vidal even sends Warren to a male
brothel, where Glenellen purchases a handsome
youth for him and leaves him to his pleasure, very
much to Warren's embarrassment and Vidal's arch
amusement:

It would be startling to report that the stalwart Philip suc-
cumbed to pagan vice, that the habits of his maturity were
in an instant undone by this classic figure which, against his
will, he found himself admiring. But we must remain true
to the fact of Philip's character and report, truthfully, that
nothing happened.

Vidal's fine impudence vis-à-vis the conventional aesthetics of the novel is particularly evident in his
revival of three characters from earlier novels—Robert Holton from *In a Yellow Wood,* Jim Willard from
The City and the Pillar, and Charles de Cluny from
Dark Green, Bright Red—all of whom play insignifi-
cant roles in *The Judgment of Paris.* It is Vidal's
tongue-in-cheek conceit, I suspect, that he is writing
something on the order of a Faulknerian saga, a massive *roman fleuve,* perhaps. But these resuscitated

characters are so many red herrings to send us off in
search of the grand design of a life's work that has no
grand design but is rather a series of colorful moments, pleasantly and wittily arranged—rags of narrative, perhaps, but sequined rags that flash nicely on
the clothesline. In short, Vidal's talent is for the small
scene, not the large design, and for the sketch that
tends toward caricature rather than the full-dress
portrait. *The Judgment of Paris* is the first of Vidal's
novels to showcase this orientation of his narrative
gifts, and it must be accounted the first of his mature
works.[3]

    Two Sisters (1970) is also typical in several ways
of Vidal's *oeuvre* but at a higher level of art than *The
Judgment of Paris*. Subtitled "A Novel in the Form
of a Memoir" on its jacket and subtitled teasingly "A
Memoir in the Form of a Novel" on its title page, the
story is related by an autobiographical V. who dallies
with a former mistress named Marietta Donegal in
Rome in 1968. After they discuss the critics' reaction
to *Myra Breckinridge*, V.'s most recent novel, the
former lovers reminisce about Paris in the 1940s and
about a pair of extraordinarily beautiful twins, Eric
and Erika Van Damm, who were among their acquaintances at the time. Marietta has in her possession a film script which the recently deceased Eric
had written in 1948, and V. reads it at her request,
together with Eric's journal, to judge whether it is
worth the $100,000 Marietta hopes to command for
it. *Two Sisters* consequently takes the form of nested
stories. At its center is the complete text of Eric's
screenplay, entitled "Two Sisters of Ephesus"; en-
veloping the screenplay is the text of Eric's 1948
journal, which is addressed to Erika; and enclosing
both is V.'s narrative, which not only frames Eric's
manuscripts but regularly interrupts them so that V.

can interject a query, a differing recollection, or an anecdote.

Eric's screenplay is set in the fourth century B.C. and deals with the sibling rivalry of Helena, a widow of the Great King of Persia, and Artemisa, the widow of a demoted Carian satrap. The various attempts of the two sisters each to outshine the other reach a climax when Artemisa announces her imminent marriage to Achoris, the richest man in the world. Helena is indignant because she had been planning to marry Achoris herself, and to upstage her sister she therefore commits suicide. But Eric shifts the focus of the screenplay at this point to the sisters' half brother, Herostratus, who has been conspiring to free Ephesus from Persian domination. When Herostratus realizes that his sisters' rivalry has led to the betrayal of his conspiracy, he avenges himself by setting fire to the Temple of Diana during Artemisa's nuptials, thereby outstripping the sisters' bid for notoriety with a more egregious bid of his own. "So remember me, that I do not die," he intones solemnly to future generations at the end of the film script. "Forget the two sisters of Ephesus for what are they but simply witnesses to Herostratus? who burned the temple of Diana which was the wonder of the earth."

Eric's journal deals with situations as exotic as those in the film script. He talks in veiled terms about a standoff with V., who would like to share Eric's bed but has to settle for Erika's, and he talks in terms even more veiled about his incestuous relationship with Erika, with whom he has fathered a child. In a lighter vein, he talks about his dealings with a libidinous Hollywood mogul named Morris Murray, who wants to turn "Two Sisters of Ephesus" into a bubble-bath classic.

But the immediate impact of *Two Sisters* derives

not so much from its miscellaneous exotica as from
the reader's sense that the novel is a *roman à clef.* V.
is of course Vidal himself, and the novel is replete
with autobiographical allusions to the novels Vidal
has written, to his more established opinions, and to
his family and friends. Many of these allusions have
the charm of self-parody. Eric notes in his journal, for
instance, that "V. is as sharp about the motives of
others as he is evasive about his own," and V. is several times brought up short by Eric's low opinion of
Vidal's novels. V. even serves up the Bouvier sisters,
Jacqueline Onassis and Lee Radziwill, with whom
Vidal shares a stepfather. In an allusion to Nina Auchincloss Steers, to whom the novel is dedicated, he
says:

As if being my sister was not sufficient burden she is also
stepsister to the two most successful adventuresses of our
time. For someone with a virtuous (in the ancient sense)
disposition, to be associated with that never-ending soap
opera is a curious punishment. She is also the heroine of a
droll revision of the Cinderella story: the two wicked stepsisters move in and take over Cinderella's house; then one
marries Prince Charming and the other marries a second
Prince Charming, leaving Cinderella to settle down to a
quiet life with a good citizen.

   The sisters Bouvier, however, receive much less
attention on the *roman à clef* level of the novel than
the diarist Anaïs Nin, one of Vidal's early friends in
the literary establishment and the model for Marietta Donegal. Marietta talks at length about releasing
the inhibitions and about "flowing" as a mode of life,
very much in Nin's vague manner, and all the confidences Marietta seeks out are so much raw material
for her public diary, just as such confidences were for
Nin. "To be candid with Marietta means to be fixed
for all times in the distorting aspic of her prose," V.

observes wryly, and Vidal takes his revenge for Nin's disclosure of some of his confidences[4] by suggesting that Marietta's fame is based on a lifetime of kiss and tell:

At eighty she will still be making love and writing about it in that long autobiography which begins with our century and will, I am certain, last well into the next for, like it or not, we live in *her* age—was she not the mistress of D. H. Lawrence (two volumes hardly described the three—or was it four?—times she bedded that ensorcelled genius) as well as the beloved inspiration—and brutal seducer—of so many other writers, painters, sculptors and even one President, though whether it was sunrise or sunset at Campobello has never been entirely clear (out of admiration for Eleanor Roosevelt she has yet to give us the entire story).

Other celebrities are alluded to under their real names in anecdotes that one presumes are sketched from life. "Of all the power-lovers I have known Eleanor Roosevelt was the most divided and so the most interesting," V. comments, and he goes on to tell of a dinner party celebrating the fall of Carmine de Sapio at which Mrs. Roosevelt revealed a surprising vengefulness. An anecdote Vidal tells about the "beat" novelist Jack Kerouac set the gossip columns humming. "I have usually found that whenever I read about an occasion where I was present, the report (except once) never tallies with my own," he says as a prelude to elaborating that anecdote—an occasion described by Kerouac in *The Subterraneans* (1958) and perfectly recalled, V. says, "until the crucial moment when Jack and I went to bed together at the Chelsea Hotel." An especially bewitching anecdote commemorates Vidal's visit to André Gide in 1948; another commemorates a still-extant brothel Marcel Proust set up for an Algerian boy friend.

Because it is host to a wealth of such anecdotes

and allusions, *Two Sisters,* like *The Judgment of Paris,*
is vintage Vidal. But because the novel's plot, typically, is almost swamped by such asides, one must wonder whether Vidal is at heart an essayist, as many of
his critics theorize. It is undeniable, I suppose, that
one of the greatest pleasures of Vidal's fiction is the
fine essayistic excursus. One enjoys the asides on Eleanor Roosevelt and on the brothels of Paris, for instance, quite independently of the novels that
embody them; the urbane rendering of the asides is
a complete and sufficient pleasure. If the pleasure of
such moments were all that *Two Sisters* offered, one
would have to agree that Vidal mistakes his genre.

But the novel's plot is not quite swamped by
asides, and *Two Sisters* is somewhat more than an
anthology of fine essayistic excursus, as it is somewhat
more than a *roman à clef.* The novel makes a firm
appeal to the aesthetic sense inasmuch as the screenplay, Eric's journal, and V.'s commentary echo each
other to such a degree that the three narratives seem
to replicate a single story line. Herostratus's relationship to Helena echoes Eric's relationship to Erika, for
instance, and Vidal's evident affection for his half
sister strikes a resonant chord on the auctorial level.
The Bouvier rivalry echoes significantly with the
Helena-Artemisa rivalry, especially when we recall
that Artemisa marries the richest man in the world
after a resonant widowhood; and Herostratus has
even aspired to be a playwright, like Eric and like
Vidal. A motif of fiery death is of especial importance
in unifying the three levels of the narrative. Just as
Herostratus's setting fire to Diana's temple is tantamount to committing suicide, so Eric apparently
commits suicide by plunging into a burning building,
as if his fictional surrogate had enacted his fate before
him. There is even a passage in which V. dreams of
his father, cremated the winter before, and sees

bright flames where his eyes should have been. "Ultimate fate of watery creatures in a fiery universe," he
murmurs in epitaph, and in the last paragraph of the
novel he reflects on Eric's death in a way that suggests that these fiery correspondences are the novel's
central point:

So at the end, fire. What else? For the three of us and all
the others, too, when time stops and the fiery beast falls
upon itself to begin again as dust-filled wind, without memory or you, Herostratus.

In light of such correspondences, we must conclude that the story of Herostratus and his sisters is
the transposed story of Eric and Erika and that the
story of V. and Marietta is the transposed story of
Vidal and his stepsisters. The correspondences are
loose, but no looser than the *roman à clef* correspondences, and the looseness of these large correspondences seems to be a contrived effect, suggesting
what the mirroring subtitles of the novel hint: that
any novel—*Two Sisters* in particular—is virtually a
hall of mirrors, with a lonely auctorial self flashing
agitated signals down the corridors of memory and
imagination. Whether the author is created by his
own imagination, or the other way around, is his unresolved problem. That the characters are only his
projections of himself is a disturbing possibility. A
terrible sense of metaphysical loss is the burden of
the auctorial condition, Vidal seems to say, for the
agitated flashing of reflections—memoir to novel and
novel to memoir, each tending to transmute into the
other—involves an irredeemable loss of everything
that is private and personal. Indeed, the novel has its
most telling moments in passages that eulogize losses
tantamount to the loss of self—the suicide of Eric, the
death of Vidal's father, the end of youth:

Death, summer, youth—this triad contrives to haunt me
every day of my life for it was in summer that my generation left school for war, and several dozen that one knew
(but strictly speaking did not love, except perhaps for one)
were killed, and so never lived to know what I have known
—the Beatles, black power, the Administration of Richard
Nixon—all this has taken place in a trivial after-time and
has nothing to do with anything that really mattered, with
summer and someone hardly remembered, a youth—not
Eric—so abruptly translated from vivid, well-loved (if
briefly) flesh to a few scraps of bone and cartilage scattered
among the volcanic rocks of Iwo Jima. So much was cruelly
lost and one still mourns the past, particularly in darkened
movie houses, weeping at bad films, or getting drunk alone
while watching the Late Show on television as our summer's war is again refought and one sees sometimes what
seems to be a familiar face in the battle scenes—is it Jimmy? But the image is promptly replaced and one will never
know whether it was he or only a member of the Screen
Actors Guild, now grown old, too.[5]

The ultimate subject of *Two Sisters* is dividedness. Just as V. longs fruitlessly for union with Eric,
his auctorial alter ego, so Eric longs for union with
Erika, his feminine alter ego, and with Herostratus,
his activist alter ego, and so on, ad infinitum; all
modes of such longing reflect the cravings of Plato's
animus for a wholeness dimly recalled. Dividedness
seems to subsume almost every aspect of *Two Sisters*
and of Vidal's entire *oeuvre*. The struggle of Vidal's
essayistic moments against his narrative forms is perhaps its ultimate foregrounding, but dividedness sub-
sumes as well the yearning of his characters to
overcome their inevitable estrangement from one
another, the aspiration of his adults to touch again
the dead hand of childhood, the instinctive attraction
of his dispassionate observers to his men of power,
and the clash in his own manner between the prankster and the pundit.

It must be remembered, however, that this dialectic is itself only one half of Vidal's art. The civilized high jinks, the mordant *roman à clef,* and the anecdotal billets-doux remain a vital part of *Two Sisters, The Judgment of Paris,* and the great body of Vidal's fiction. Half grimace, half high spirits, the wry smile is Vidal's most telling expression.

The mix of ingredients in *Kalki* (1978) is also typical of Vidal's fiction, although the novel is somewhat less successful than *Two Sisters* or even *The Judgment of Paris.* The narrator of this doomsday odyssey is Teddy Ottinger, a plainspoken, bisexual aviatrix, a feminist who can boast of cauterized tubes, alimony payments to her ex-husband, and a best-selling autobiography, *Beyond Motherhood.* Because she is behind in her alimony payments, Teddy agrees at her agent's behest to fly to India and interview James J. Kelly, a Vietnam veteran who has styled himself "Kalki" and claims to be the last avatar of the Hindu god Vishnu. Ever vulnerable to physical beauty, Teddy is quickly smitten by the golden blondness of both Kalki and his wife Lakshmi, the former Doris Pannicker. Vaguely in love with the two of them, she is persuaded to sign on as Kalki's personal pilot and to become part of a cadre that includes Geraldine O'Connor, an MIT biochemist, and Giles Lowell, a medical doctor also known as R. S. Ashok, Ph.D. Kalki declares that the five of them are Perfect Masters and will preside over the end of the world when Siva the Destroyer, one of Vishnu's manifestations, brings human life to an end. He even sets a precise date for doomsday—April 3.

Teddy is more difficult to seduce intellectually than aesthetically, however, and she retains deep misgivings about Kalki and his cult, not only because of her atheism but because of persistent rumors that the cult camouflages a major drug operation. The cult is indeed supported by drug sales, but Kalki sincerely believes that he is Vishnu, and he fully intends to terminate human life. After a major publicity campaign, including the elaborately staged murder of a Kalki look-alike, Kalki performs Siva's Dance of Eternity on April 3; when he is finished, everyone in the world is dead except for the five Perfect Masters. Teddy later discovers that she was the agent of death. On Kalki's orders, she had spread a lethal bacteria throughout the world via her airplane without knowing what she was doing. Like the other Perfect Masters, she survives the virus because she had been inoculated against its effects.

The five survivors organize their subsequent lives first in New York, then in Paris, and finally in Washington, where Kalki and Lakshmi take up residence in the White House. Gradually, Teddy realizes the fullness of Kalki's mad plot. Because Giles, Geraldine, and she are all sterile, Kalki and Lakshmi will be the parents of a new human race, and Kalki will thus play Vishnu the Creator as well as Siva the Destroyer. But Giles, the villain of the novel, has another scenario in mind. He carefully neglects to inform Kalki and Lakshmi that their blood types are incompatible, and after their first child is stillborn, he further neglects the steps necessary to ensure the safety of future births. Not really sterile at all, he plans to replace Kalki in Lakshmi's bed and himself father the new race. Kalki kills him as soon as he realizes the situation, however, thereby ending all hopes for the continuation of the species. The four survivors live out their life spans quietly, with Teddy working on the written record that is the novel. Kalki is the last to die, as he tells us in a postscript to Teddy's text. In a last gesture of divine magnanimity, he bequeaths Earth to the monkeys.

As this synopsis suggests, *Kalki* is a very modish novel. Laboratory-controlled genetics, ecological disaster, jet-set travel, entropy, Eastern religions, birth control, bisexuality, violence, drugs, feminist tracts, Walter Cronkite presiding benignly over the mix—*Kalki* has them all. As an aviatrix with no fear of flying, Teddy seems to be reconstituted from Erica Jong's popular novel *Fear of Flying* (1973), and the Kalki cult suggests in many ways the followers of the Korean evangelist Sun Myung Moon who were so much in evidence during the 1970s.

This modishness tends to create satiric effects even when it is merely true to life. Teddy's mother-in-law is rather proud of the possibility that she has cancer, for instance, regarding the "Big C" as a status symbol outranking even the "Big O" in the alphabetics of the decade. Hollywood's most successful pitch-woman has a gallbladder-shaped pool with imitation gallstones on the bottom—a play on kidney-shaped pools, circa 1940, in the overdone style of 1970s wit. A technical director of the television show *60 Minutes* assures Teddy that he is giving Kalki's doomsday announcement major attention, "maybe ten, ten and a half, maybe even eleven minutes, you know, an in-depth study." Government agencies are satirized more cavalierly though not untowardly. Both the Drug Enforcement Administration and its watchdog committee in the Senate have as their goal the increased sale of drugs all over the world, we are assured, since without such enterprise they would not be funded. CIA agents misrepresent themselves so consistently that Teddy is willing to believe that Giles is *not* with the CIA only when he says that he *is*. An IRS accountant explains, somewhat madly, "We at the IRS never assume that anyone is innocent until he is proven guilty."

Because this preposterous farrago is essentially

the 1970s scene, hardly exaggerated at all, Vidal
seems to be following the principle laid down by
some black humorists that contemporary realities are
so innately absurd that to write comic fantasy one
need only straightforwardly report things as they
are. Certainly Vidal has never done less to enhance
his satire than in this novel. The stylized syntax that
focuses a satiric point, the commentary that elabo-
rates the point, lending it emphasis, grace, and dispassion, all the rhetorical tricks that make Vidal's
usual satire a deadly but elegant cocktail are es-
chewed in *Kalki* in favor of mere exposure—murder
by suicide, as it were. It is a valid technique, of
course, especially for a humorist in a black mood, for
it suggests that things as they are merit neither wit
nor stylization. It is ultimately a nihilistic kind of
satire, perhaps the most difficult kind to achieve successfully.

Teddy Ottinger is an appropriate vehicle for
such satire, for she is determinedly unsentimental
and carefully unfeeling, as bland a consciousness as a
nihilist could wish. Meeting her ex-husband after a
long interval, she says,

I must have felt *something* for him once, I thought, staring
through the martini's first comforting haze at my ex-husband's pale double chin.

Tears came to my eyes. There were tears in his eyes,
too. Love? Tenderness? Regret? No. It was the red-alert
smog, creeping up the Santa Monica canyon from the Pa-
cific Freeway.

On being told that she has killed 4 billion people,
Teddy's only reaction is to look in a mirror and check
that her face is suitably blank, although she confesses
later to a modest depression. It is perhaps not surprising that she considers herself "in heat" rather than
"in love" when she thinks of Kalki, but it is surprising

that for all her vaunted love of flying, she never once
conveys the ecstasy of flight. Vidal quashes all vibran-
cy in Teddy because if she were more vital, she
would be less likely to think the Earth well rid of her
kind. But as it is, Teddy and Geraldine sit in New
York City's Bryant Park shortly before The End and
watch a "parade of monsters" that Teddy happily
consigns to oblivion:

Drunk, drugged, mad, they staggered past us, talking to
themselves. I thought it very apt that on a building opposite us was one of the KALKI, THE END billboards. I could
not imagine any of these people wanting to go on.

In fact, Teddy's assent to Kalki's genocide is implicit in a number of her remarks: "But then [if I
were God] I would not have gone to the trouble of
inventing the human race"; "I did not believe that
Kalki would switch off the human race . . . as desir-
able a happening as that might be." Like Vidal, she
sees no point to a world in which matrons pride
themselves on their cancer operations and derelicts
await the apocalypse on park benches. Nothing is
really worth saving, she believes, and the novel goes
beyond the usual limits of doomsday fiction, therefore, by saving nothing, not even Teddy.

A nihilistic point of view is never far from the
surface of Vidal's art, but nowhere else in the *oeuvre*
is it expressed by such an understated technique.
And if *Kalki* is less successful than the other novels
of Vidal's maturity, the reason is simply that its low
intensity is inconsistent with Vidal's gifts, which run
to high style and flashing wit. Too many of *Kalki*'s
modish allusions waste a satiric potential. The Kat-
mandu ashram is wired with muzak, but Teddy's
only response is to observe that the tapes are out of
date. The enervating blandness of the muzak receives no verbal attention, nor does its inappropri-

ateness in a Hindu monastery, although Vidal surely intends these points to score satirically. Similarly, when the five survivors meet to plan the education of the next generation, they agree immediately to reject the new math but plan no further. Fair enough, perhaps, but is it really enough? As one longs to have Vidal elaborate on the vapidness of the muzak, so one longs for him to strike sparks from the new-math debacle and to devise a total education that would savage contemporary schooling.

One always has the impression that the text of *Kalki* is straining to escape its straightforward manner. In particular, Vidal is unable to resist adding touches to Teddy's character that are ultimately functionless yet suggest that she might have been more interesting had her nihilistic straitjacket allowed it. Teddy is a great fan of Antoine de Saint-Exupéry's aviation literature, for instance, and she agrees with his interesting notion that the natural aviator is a fascist, determined to be outside, above, and beyond the human race. Does she then secretly long for Kalki's apocalypse because it places her in this superior position? Is her expressed distaste both for the apocalypse and for continued existence hypocritical? Teddy is also a devotee of the aviatrix Amelia Earhart, which on the face of things is natural enough, but she also dreams that Earhart is her mother. Her real mother, an embittered, jealous woman, committed suicide the day Teddy won a prestigious aviation trophy, and so Earhart is clearly her mother's surrogate. Thus, when we are told that Teddy started sleeping with older women after her mother's death, we assume that she was both reaching out to her dead mother and searching for Earhart.

Complicating this strand of meaning still further, Vidal tends to merge with Teddy, for he too was

estranged from his mother, and his father was one of
Earhart's friends. Is Vidal foregrounding himself,
then, and admitting to a wish fantasy that Earhart
were *his* mother? Conceivably, but as soon as one
admits such provocative strands of meaning in the
text of *Kalki*, things fall apart. One demands a connection that does not exist between Teddy's search
for a mother and her involvement with Kalki. One
demands a more elaborate connection between Teddy's fly-girl fascism and the coolness with which she
faces The End. One demands a connection, more
autobiographically explicable, between Vidal and his
fiction.

The novel's style has something of the same
problem. Teddy is acutely aware of the clichés with
which her prose is burdened and apologizes for them
ad nauseam, as if the deterioration of language alone
justified man's extermination. Yet her narrative has
moments of stylistic gold. About the end of the
human race, for instance, Teddy says with eloquent
simplicity, "You cannot mourn everyone. Only someone." And in a rare moment of wit she remarks, "I
was able to read the odd page by Joan Didion, the
even page by Renata Adler," efficiently making the
point that she can read neither.

This failure of *Kalki* to abide by its chosen inelo-
quence suggests once again that Vidal's genius is for
the quick effect, not the sustained technique, for the
clothesline, not the story line. Typically, the larger
techniques of *Kalki* fall prey to Vidal's impulses of
the moment, and so we have those sudden elabora-
tions of character and golden phrases that are marvelous in themselves but discountenance the ploys of
the larger fiction. Perhaps this is why Vidal's first-
person narratives are generally more successful than
his third-person narratives and why the imaginary
journal, requiring so little in the way of plot, has

proven his most successful narrative form, *Kalki* excepted. In short, Vidal's particular gifts demand an open narrative form that will host many narrative postures. Think of the joke about the chameleon suffering a nervous breakdown on a bolt of plaid cloth. Because he is a sort of chameleon, Vidal is equally at odds with intricate patterns.

3.
The Early Successes:
Williwaw, The City and the Pillar

Vidal resolved early in his life to be a novelist, and he has quietly sustained that resolve over the years, never affecting to be driven by a vision, to be haunted by Scheherazade, or to be anything other than a workaday professional. But like any other novelist, Vidal needed time and experience to find his own voices; and like many writers of his generation, he fell under the sway of Hemingway's voice before sounding his own. In general, his early, imitative works are not impressive. Two novels among them stand out, however: *Williwaw*, his first novel and a *succès d'estime*, and *The City and the Pillar*, his third novel and a *succès de scandale*.

Williwaw (1946) draws heavily on Vidal's personal experiences. The novel was begun in the winter of 1944–45 while he was serving as first mate on an Army freight ship en route between Chernowski Bay and Dutch Harbor in the Aleutian Islands, and *Williwaw* is set aboard a similar freight ship plying a wartime path from Andrefski Bay to Arunga in the same Aleutian chain at the same time of year. The first mate in Vidal's novel is even an auctorial portrait. He has a "carefully studied collegiate manner though he had never been to a college"; he is "dark and nearly handsome"; his voice is "deep, interesting, and mocking"; and he is as inadequate a first mate as Vidal admits he was himself.

The novel has seven main characters. Warrant Officer Evans is the ship's master, John Martin is the first mate, Duval is the chief engineer, and Bervick is the second mate. There are three passengers: Major Barkison, the highest-ranking officer; Lieutenant Hodges, his aide; and Father O'Mahoney, a Catholic chaplain. The interaction of these seven men does not constitute a plot so much as a narrative texture thick with antagonism. Evans is quick to remind Martin of his incompetence as a first mate, and Evans is piqued in return by Martin's mocking tone and show of popularity with the crew. Jealous of Evans's seamanship, Major Barkison encourages gossip that minimizes Evans's skill, and Barkison is dismayed in his turn that Hodges detects his motion sickness. Duval annoys Evans with his troublemaking, Evans annoys the chaplain with his religious indifference, and the chaplain annoys everyone with his too-personal queries.

But the rivalry of Bervick and Duval over a prostitute who lives in Dutch Harbor is the most violent of the antagonisms; shortly after the williwaw, Bervick throws a hammer at Duval, causing him to lose his balance, fall overboard, and drown. No one initially suspects Bervick's involvement in the drowning. When his involvement becomes clear, everyone dismisses it casually, even Barkison, who is charged with the official inquiry into Duval's death. The novel ends with an insidious quiet that is an extension of this unconcern: the ship headed for drydock under a blue sky and a bright sun, the several antagonisms muted.

Much of *Williwaw* deals with falling barometers and mounting waves, of course, but the williwaw

itself is a tempered element in the novel. It is not
rendered in the high color of most storms in literature of the sea, and it is not rendered directly but
rather through the crew's experience. Yet the williwaw functions importantly in the narrative structure. Its natural violence is a loose analogue to the
human violence aboard ship, its classically plotted
development lends shape to the antagonisms that
texture the novel, and the restraint with which the
williwaw is depicted foreshadows the low-keyed
treatment of Duval's death. Indeed, Duval drowns in
the calm following the williwaw rather than at the
height of the storm, although sea literature is filled
with precedents in which such events occur together, with nature reinforcing the human drama. Vidal
will have no part of such hyperbole. Restraint is the
hallmark of *Williwaw*, its style and its distinction.

This stylistic restraint allows individual scenes to
realize themselves with a subtlety that a *Sturm und
Drang* treatment would have overwhelmed. In a
particularly subtle scene, Duval muses critically on
the chaplain's inability to perform any practical
tasks. As if his sensitive ego had registered this un-
spoken criticism, the chaplain turns suddenly to
Hodges and asks, "Are you Catholic?" needing to
upstage someone, anyone, with his single distinction.
Equally subtle dynamics shape a scene just after the
ship survives the williwaw. The crew sit at table,
congratulating Evans on the ship's survival, while
Duval simmers with envy. Duval then cries out,
"Pass the sugar," an unconsciously symbolic request
that Evans unconsciously registers, moving him to
turn a share of the praise Duval's way. Many such
scenes have a fine subtlety of detail, as when Major
Barkison enquires whether Evans is quite competent
while he unconsciously sketches cartoons of sinking
ships and when Bervick contrives his story about Du-

val's death while Hodges builds an elaborate house of
cards.

The terse, realistic dialogue of *Williwaw* is well
adapted to such scenes, but it is usually criticized as
an unsuccessful imitation of Hemingway's style.[1] The
Hemingway influence is undeniable, but neither
Vidal's technique nor his focus is entirely the same as
Hemingway's. The following passage is illustrative:

Loud music startled them. The Chaplain looked about him
apologetically and quickly lowered the volume. "Finally
got some music," he announced. "The static isn't so bad
tonight."

The Major agreed, "Yes, the static's not bad at all tonight."

The Lieutenant remarked that the static had been bad
the night before.

That, thought Martin, takes care of the static. He often
wondered why people spoke so inanely.

Had Hemingway written this passage, he would
have omitted Martin's final commentary and allowed
the conversation to seem desperate and compulsive.
By rendering Martin stonily unthoughtful, Hemingway would have implied further that wracked nerves
stood behind Martin's blankness. But Vidal makes
the speakers seem dim-witted and Martin seem
merely irritable by having Martin *reflect* that the
conversation is inane. The difference is fundamental.
Whereas Hemingway's technique is one of implica-
tion and focuses on psychological depths, Vidal's
technique in *Williwaw* is one of explication and
focuses on psychic surfaces.

Psychic surfaces are the true subject of *Williwaw,* for all the characters are poseurs without feeling for anything but the faces they show to the world.
Evans, for example, has a fond but absurd interest in
his own profile. "He had seen it once in a tailor's

three-way mirror," we are told. "He had been greatly interested, and he hoped vaguely that he might
see it again sometime." Major Barkison has a similar
interest, convinced that nature has blessed him with
the Duke of Wellington's profile. "Knowing this, he
hoped that someone might someday mention the
resemblance; no one ever did." Undaunted, however, the major is given to striking heroic poses, and
he even dreams of playing Wellington on the stage.
His daydreams are so adolescent that Hodges finds
them silly, yet Hodges himself affects a cold and
severe look in imitation of the major's imitation of
Wellington.

Indeed, the novel is filled with actors and would-
be actors. Before his induction into the Army, Martin
was "one of the numerous unpromising young actors
in a New England stock company," and he affects
aboard ship a studied collegiate manner. With valid
cause, both Martin and Bervick find Evans something of an actor, affectedly blasé, liking to play at
authority. The chaplain, we are told, "acted as if he
were playing a part in a bad dream, and perhaps he
was." He is surely the most dreary of the poseurs,
with a particular fondness for confiding his "revela-
tions" during moments of stress. In one of the most
pitiless scenes in the book, he announces ponderous-
ly that the williwaw has purged him forever of jealousy and fear of death, only to manifest both of those
feelings nakedly a moment later.

Vidal implies a link between the self-absorption
of these men and the indifference they show to Duval's death and to Bervick's guilt, and he also implies
a link to their larger failures in marriage and career.
The williwaw must therefore be understood as a test
of their self-absorption. Can it displace their concern
with face? Advance to the foreground of their awareness? Not really. Evans worries during the williwaw

about what will be said of him if he loses his ship, the major and the chaplain worry about their stomachs disgracing them, and Martin is blissfully unaware of everything, having accidentally been knocked unconscious. No one discovers in the raw power of the storm something greater than his selfhood; no one reaches communal awareness through an act of heroism. Each man suffers the storm alone.

That nineteen-year-old Gore Vidal should have been capable of writing *Williwaw* is astonishing. Most first novels suffer from overstuffing, as if the writers were compelled to cram all the performance of which they are capable into a first, definitive work. *Williwaw* is distinctive among such novels for its restraint. It is also astonishing that a young man who was something of a poseur himself should have been capable of writing with detachment about the posturing of the young and the insecure. It is most astonishing of all that young Vidal should have recognized that he had neither the sensibility nor the elaborate technique of Hemingway at this early point in his career and that he should consequently have taken from Hemingway only a technique of sketching brittle human surfaces. *Williwaw* is atypical of Vidal's best work, but it is an outstanding first novel, and it remains an important work in the Vidal *oeuvre*.

If *Williwaw* is distinguished among first novels for its restraint, *The City and the Pillar* (1948, revised 1965) is notable for its boldness. "I was bored with playing it safe," Vidal wrote in an afterword. "I wanted to take risks, to try something no American had done before." And so he wrote what had never been published by a reputable American writer: an unreserved novel about the homosexual demimonde and the "naturalness" of homosexual relations. Readers, reviewers, and advertisers were predictably

offended. The novel sold well because it was sensational, but it was sensational to a degree that obviat-
ed consideration of its literary quality, and many
readers came to believe that Vidal was confessing a
seamy underside to his life. "To this day," he remarks, "aging pederasts are firmly convinced that I
was once a male prostitute, with an excellent back-
hand at tennis." In 1965 Vidal published a revised
edition of the novel, changing the ending, tightening
the style, removing a number of moralizing passages,
and adding the afterword—all in an effort to gain
more serious consideration for a work indissolubly
linked to his reputation. This greatly improved version of the novel is the version considered here.

The hero of *The City and the Pillar* is Jim Willard, a shy, likable young man with a proficient game
of tennis, good looks, and a best friend named Bob
Ford who is one year ahead of him in school. The two
youths experience sex together during an idyllic
weekend in the Virginia woods just before Ford is
graduated and goes off to sea. The experience is "awful kid stuff" to Ford, but it is the fulfillment of Willard's secret dream. Thus, he goes to sea himself a
year later in the hope of a romantic reunion, although he has no idea of Ford's whereabouts or
whether Ford wants a reunion. Willard does not
think of himself as homosexual at this time or even
after he drifts to Hollywood and becomes the kept
lover of a film star named Ronald Shaw, for he remains emotionally faithful to Ford, whom he thinks
of euphemistically as a lost "twin" and "ideal brother."

But Willard gradually moves deeper into the
homosexual world. He passes from a shallow involvement with Shaw to a deeper involvement with a
writer named Paul Sullivan, and he passes with Sullivan into something of a *menage à trois* with Maria

Verlaine, a woman who accompanies them on a Mex-
ican jaunt. Inducted into the Army after Pearl Harbor, he spends his time fighting off a homosexual
sergeant while attempting to seduce a handsome
corporal, and after his discharge he becomes en-
meshed once again in the New York demimonde of
Sullivan and Verlaine. Bob Ford remains his "ideal
brother" throughout.

Bob Ford suddenly returns home to be married.
At the climax of the book, Willard tries to seduce
him, despite all the evidence that Ford is heterosexual, and he rapes Ford cruelly when he is spurned.[2]
The story concludes as it began, with a disillusioned
Willard sitting quietly in a bar after his *crime passionel*, a figurative pillar of salt looking hypnotically to
a city of Sodom set deep in the Virginia woods. Like
the wife of Lot, he is the sad victim of an unfortunate
backward glance, and "a memory of bruised flesh,
tangled sheets, violence" finally supplants the memory of his lover and ideal brother.

The City and the Pillar evokes a number of texts
in American literature. Preeminently, Jim Willard
calls to mind George Willard, the protagonist of Sherwood Anderson's *Winesburg, Ohio* (1919). Willard
evokes some of Mark Twain's characters, too, sometimes playing Tom Sawyer to Ford's Huck Finn and
sometimes playing Huck Finn to Ford's Nigger Jim.
More subtly, Willard is reminiscent of Nick Adams in
Hemingway's *In Our Time* (1924) and of Eugene
Gant in Thomas Wolfe's *Look Homeward, Angel*
(1929). One could go on to identify echoes of any
number of young men in such works, for Jim Willard
is a stereotypical character in American literature,
one of those boy-men who walk dim-wittedly among
persons more emotionally engaged than themselves,
until a climactic scene in which they discover in
themselves an unprecedented measure of emotion.

Willard is also one of those boy-men of American literature who focus their emotion upon other males.[3] Willard's passion for Bob Ford recalls Natty Bumppo's affection for Chingachgook, Ishmael's love for Queequeg, Huck Finn's care for Nigger Jim, and Nick Carraway's feeling for Gatsby. In short, Jim Willard is a mainstream character, and his fixation on Bob Ford is embedded deep in the mainstream culture.

This mainstream depiction naturally made Willard offensive to that majority of people in 1948 who thought homosexuals should be depicted as empurpled aesthetes. But it must be noted that Vidal's representation of mainstream homosexuality had a certain cachet in 1948, for many of the statistics of the forthcoming Kinsey Report were bruited months before the appearance of *The City and the Pillar*, and a shocked public was just beginning to realize, via Kinsey, that one out of three males has homosexual experience during adolescence and that one out of ten males is homosexual.[4] In its depiction of mainstream homosexuality, then, *The City and the Pillar* shared in the ground-breaking candor of the Kinsey Report as well as in its notoriety.

But *The City and the Pillar* is not the Kinsey Report, content simply to suggest the incidence of homosexuality. Essentially, *The City and the Pillar* is about the experience of discovering that one is homosexual, and it depicts especially the labyrinth which that experience can seem. Vidal records wryly, for instance, the remarks and questions that disturb Willard's homosexual sensitivities: his younger brother observing that he never goes out with girls, a friend asking why he didn't go to the graduation dance, his family elaborating coyly the joys of marriage. And Vidal records in detail Willard's care to conceal his homosexual inclination even from him-

self. Willard is scrupulously careful not to show too
much pleasure in Bob Ford's company and not to
initiate the sexual play in the woods. When he accompanies his California friends to homosexual gath-
erings, he plays at being heterosexual, "to
experience," he pretends, "the pleasure of saying
no." He steadfastly refuses to see a connection between what he and Ford did in the woods and what
his homosexual friends do, and as Shaw's lover he
affects to retain heterosexual integrity by refusing to
say that he loves Shaw. "The idea of being in love
with a man was both ludicrous and unnatural," he
thinks. "At the most a man might find his twin, like
Bob, but that was rare and something else again."
Even after he knows that he is homosexual, Willard
half believes that "should he ever have a woman he
would be normal." "There was not much to base this
hope on," Vidal tells us coolly, "but he believed it."

Yet his attraction to men and his concomitant
distaste for women distress Willard very little. What
distresses him is the homosexual stigma. Maria Verlaine asks him, "Do you mind it very much, being
different?" and he *hates* her, we are told, because she
had "marked" him. In a kindred scene, Willard attempts to take a woman to bed while a friend named
Collins beds her roommate. The attempt is a fiasco.
As he runs in defeat from the room, Willard is embarrassed by Collins crying out, "Let the queer go! I got
enough for two." The word "queer" haunts Willard
thereafter much more than the memory of his sexual
incapacity, for it is another mark of his homosexuality. The insulting word becomes "what Collins had
called him" in his mind, and his distaste for the marking is so intense that he childishly suppresses the
word. Significantly, Ford also calls Willard "queer"
just before Willard vengefully rapes him.

Such foolishness makes Willard seem very bland.

Indeed, the absence of a more profound response to
his homosexuality makes him seem vacuous, half
formed, and insubstantial, and Vidal throws this aspect of Willard into sharp relief by depicting other
characters in the novel more crisply. Willard's father,
for instance, is virtually caricatured as the man who
compensates for professional failure by tyrannizing
his family, and his mother is the classic martyr to a
bad marriage. Bob Ford is indubitably the dumb ox;
Ronald Shaw, the narcissist; Maria Verlaine, the
femme fatale; Paul Sullivan, the emotional masoch-
ist. All the main characters, then, are drawn clearly
in bright acidic colors. By Willard's comparative
blandness, Vidal suggests his protagonist's failure to
crystallize as a person. Because he judges his homosexuality by the conventional prejudices of society,
Willard denies his most essential being, and as a result he seems hollow, hardly a person at all.

Ironically, Willard has a better sense of reality
and illusion than any other character in the novel, if
we except his inability to accept homosexuality. He
knows even during his maritime period that one
should pretend to have illusions about one's friends,
and in his Hollywood period he is not deluded by
cinematic glamour as his friends are. If the core reality of the novel is that Willard has no substantial
identity, Willard knows that, too. "I don't know why
I do what I do or even who I am," he says to Maria
Verlaine. He tends even to give mirrors an inquiring
glance in passing, as if they might be able to impart
him an identity.

Vidal's very special achievement in *The City and
the Pillar* consists of the disingenuous conjunction of
all this. Willard is Everyman, and yet he is *l'étranger;*
he is less wholly realized than any other character in
the novel, yet he is the only character to escape
cliché and seem wholly authentic; he is dangerously

self-deluded, yet he is generally perceptive. The net effect is paradoxical but appropriate, for it decrees that in the last analysis we cannot patronize Jim Willard, sympathize with him entirely, or even claim to understand him. Much more so than the typical character in fiction, Jim Willard simply *exists*, not as the subject of a statement, not as the illustration of a theme, but simply as himself.

Vidal's elimination in the revised edition of *The City and the Pillar* of moralizing passages numerous in the original edition contributes greatly to this puristic effect.[5] It is surprising, then, that the author wrote a new moral for the last paragraph of the revised edition. "Nothing that ever was changes," Willard portentously summarizes. "Yet nothing that is can ever be the same as what went before." The moral is much too easy, concerned as it is with mutability and Willard's long look backward—a secondary emphasis of the novel—rather than with the homosexual emphasis that is primary, and we must adjudge it a concession to the tyranny of closure. Yet this final misemphasis is appropriate, too, for homosexuality is not a subject for moralizing in *The City and the Pillar* but only an immutable fact of Willard's existence. With the same restraint that characterizes *Williwaw*, Vidal does not deign to explore the sources of Willard's homosexuality any more than he provides a clue as to how he might deal with it. He does not even ask sympathy for Willard. The homosexuality is simply there, like Willard himself, a problem because it is made a problem.[6]

The narrative interest of *The City and the Pillar* suffers from so unbending an auctorial stance, but the novel remains absorbing after more than three decades for the intelligence of its basic tack on homosexuality and for the credibility of Jim Willard's confusion about himself. There are few novels of sensational cut about which such claims can be made three decades after they are published. Indeed, *The City and the Pillar* is one of the more important novels concerned with homosexuality. It does not bear comparison with the work of André Gide, Marcel Proust, and Thomas Mann in the European tradition of such novels, but it is certainly the most significant novel on the subject written by an American.

man, a story of Julian the Christian becoming a pagan, Julian the philosopher becoming a soldier, and Julian the prince becoming an emperor. In the first section, "Youth," the boy Julian and his half brother Gallus find themselves the sole heirs of their uncle, the Emperor Constantius. Even at this young age Julian is disenchanted with the politics that endangers his life by assuming his interest in intriguing against Constantius, and he is also disenchanted with Christianity and its bloody conflict between Arians and Athanasians. Disengaging himself from such affairs, Julian goes to Athens to embrace the quiet life of a philosophy student, although he secretly hopes to restore worship of the old gods should he one day become emperor.

In the second section, "Caesar," Gallus is appointed Caesar by Constantius, only to be executed when his ambition becomes too great. Appointed Caesar in his brother's place, Julian is immediately sent to Gaul to recapture areas taken by the Germans. Julian has no military experience, yet he succeeds brilliantly in Gaul, so impressing his men that they defy Constantius and proclaim Julian emperor. Ever a cautious man, Julian refuses to style himself Augustus and successfully avoids civil war with Constantius.

In the third section, "Augustus," Julian becomes emperor upon Constantius's death, declares a policy of religious toleration, and uses his authority to foster worship of the old gods. But Julian's genius is for military strategy, not for command, and he is no match for the maneuvering of men more venal than he. Thus, in a climactic military campaign Julian manages very nearly to conquer Persia, only to be assassinated in battle at the age of thirty-one by one of his own men.

Much that the reader might think invention in

Julian is actually historical fact. Julian's hirsuteness is
a matter of record, for instance, as are his body lice
and ink-stained fingers and his distaste for horse
races, barbers, and heated rooms. There is, in fact, no
characterizing detail or relevant anecdote in all of
the source material about the historical Julian that
Vidal failed to utilize in the novel, and he avoided the
use of merely apocryphal material, such as the words
"Thou hast conquered, O Galilean" that the historian
Theodoret attributed to the dying emperor. The
novel's historical minutiae are quite authentic; the
novel is generally authentic in such larger matters as
Christianity's debt to the mystery cults and the viper-
ous behavior of Arians and Athanasians. Imaginative
improvisation about facts is confined largely to the
existence and acquisition of Julian's manuscripts. The
result is a work of impressive historicity.

Julian's historicity is richest when Vidal bur-
nishes his fourth-century facts with his uncommon
insight. Vidal has Julian suggest that Constantius
holds himself immobile in public audiences in order
to imply the durability of a marble statue, and Julian
notes the shrewdness of that playacting in a state
given to political assassination. Vidal also has Julian
link the much-ridiculed voices of eunuchs to their
extraordinary political power under Constantius: "In
actual fact, the voice of a eunuch is like that of a
particularly gentle child, and this appeals to the par-
ent in both men and women," he says. "Thus subtly
do they disarm us, for we tend to indulge them as we
would a child, forgetting that their minds are as mature and twisted as their bodies are lacking." The
auctorial intelligence of such passages renders the
fourth century with authority and vivifies the dusty
facts of history.

But the dust of centuries mutes Vidal's story of
Julian, and many of the novel's key strategies actually

seem chosen to distance us from the story. Scenes are often summarized rather than dramatized, with a distancing effect.

There was a funny story going around at about this time, no doubt apocryphal. Julian and Macrina were overheard while making love. Apparently all during the act each one continued to talk. Macrina is supposed to have confuted the Pythagoreans while Julian restated the Platonic powers, all this before and during orgasm. They were well matched.

This summary is not without wit, but it seems undeniable that a dramatic rendering would have given it more immediacy and improved it as a scene. Sometimes the reader is distanced severely by summary, as when Julian remarks laconically of his most stirring peroration, "I will not weary the reader with a catalogue of gestures, nor every word.... I will only say that I was at my best." Why, we may ask, is Julian's best peroration suppressed while some of his lesser speeches are quoted at length? One is sometimes grateful for ellipses, of course, as on the occasions when Julian directs his secretary to append pages from his Gallic War *Commentaries* (no longer extant), for Julian thereby circumvents the necessity of describing military exploits of doubtful narrative value.

Since Vidal was fresh from a decade of experience with scripts and screenplays and their exigencies of scene and pace, one is struck by his decision to tell so much of his story by summary and at a snail's pace. One is struck, too, by a marked absence of verbal élan in the novel, for only scattered passages possess stylistic life. One must conclude that Vidal deliberately sought a muteness, a dustiness of effect, perhaps to evoke the similarly muted style of Julian's translated *Works* in the Loeb Classical Library series,[3] the standard text read by Vidal's generation. Certainly one justification for *Julian*'s workaday prose is its effect of having been translated lifelessly from the Greek.

A stylistic distinction must be maintained, however. It is Julian who is without verbal élan in the novel, not Priscus, not Libanius, and certainly not Vidal. Priscus is an accomplished phrase maker. He notes wittily of a stutterer that he "picked a word beginning with 'm' and nearly choked to death," and he remarks of a woman inhabited by the spirit of Aphrodite that she functions "rather like an inn." The pedantic Libanius has very nearly as much verbal acumen as Priscus, although his élan is that of the poseur, not the wit. His contempt for Latin in the following passage is delightfully snobbish and marvelously theatrical in its cadences; in its linking of Latin and lawyers, it is not without a contemporary edge:

Recently a student (Christian, of course) most tactfully suggested that I, Libanius, learn Latin! At my age and after a lifetime devoted to Greek! I told him that as I was not a lawyer there was nothing I needed to read in that ugly language, which has produced only one poem and that a depressing paraphrase of our great Homer.

This stylistic distinction among the narrative voices is important because it is a means by which Vidal further mutes Julian's presence in the novel. Style in Vidal is always an index to the man, and Julian's comparatively plain style renders him a less vital presence than either Priscus or Libanius, although Julian commands our attention more sustainedly. The verbal give-and-take between Priscus and Libanius makes them more vivid than Julian, too, as their repartee has exactly the abrasive, edged quality that we miss in Julian's prose. Priscus's remarks to Libanius are carefully barbed, for instance, for Priscus disdains Libanius's literary projects. "I have not had a new idea since I was twenty-seven," Priscus observes tartly, obviously believing Libanius to be as unoriginal as himself. He adds pointedly, "That is why I don't publish my lectures." Cattily, Priscus continues:

I thought I had written you about your collection of letters. I did get the book and it was very thoughtful of you to send it to me. We are all in your debt for those letters, especially yours to Julian. They are wise. I know of no other philosopher so sensible of posterity as to keep copies of *every* letter he writes, realizing that even his most trivial effusion has, in the context of the large body of his work, an external value.

Allusions to a financial disagreement and to the dysfunctions of old age are leitmotifs of the exchange between Priscus and Libanius, underscoring their indurate humanity.

Such narrative inventions humanize Julian on occasion, as when he is forced to listen to official greetings while needing desperately to relieve himself. Julian is even capable of something like wit on occasion, as when he remarks of his wife that she has the misfortune to be an "imperial portrait re-created in a middle-aged woman." But such wit on Julian's part is as ponderous as it is rare, and in general he is made to seem background to Priscus's and Libanius's foreground and to seem woodenly historical in the context of their archetypal roles as *eiron* and *alazon*, those stock figures of Greek comedy.

Yet Julian has considerable appeal both in Vidal's novel and in our general culture. Ever since the New Hellenism of the late nineteenth century, the historical Julian has been respected both as the legislator of a religious tolerance the world was not to see again until many centuries after his death and as the lonely defender of a culture more noble in its decline than upstart Christianity. He has come to symbolize, in effect, a kind of doomed political intelligence too refined for the real world. Vidal permits Julian a measured amount of this appeal because he shares Julian's liberality and anti-Christian sentiment. The logic is clearly Vidal's when one of his characters thinks it extraordinary that the absolute god of the Christians should also be a jealous god. "Jealous of what?" he wonders. With the best modern scholarship, Vidal is careful to support Julian's attacks on Christianity and its oppressions, rendering him virtually a spokesman for informed good sense as well as for Vidal himself.

Vidal grants Julian an admirable elevation of mind and a pleasant sense of self-mockery, too, even if he denies him the wit and immediacy of his commentators. Of the cloudless sky over Athens Julian aphorizes, "Attic clarity is not just metaphor; it is a fact." Called to the court of Constantius, he observes more heavily, "Wherever there is a throne, one may observe in rich detail every folly and wickedness of which man is capable, enamelled with manners and gilded with hypocrisy," and we are impressed with his grasp of imperial folly if not with the sweep of his cadences. But in a different mood Julian can observe coyly, "Now that I am Emperor, *all* my speeches are considered graceful and to the point." Of his response to the flattery of a courtier he can remark, "I lied with equal dignity," disarming us neatly. His mixture of high sentiment and self-mocking candor has its appeal.

But Vidal ambivalently undercuts this appeal of his protagonist, and this is consonant with his impulse to distance us from Julian. In early life Julian is an innocent figure, victim to his royal blood and to

Christianity's barbarisms, but as time goes on Julian's innocence is compromised. Julian himself acknowledges this after an abortive attempt to imitate the lapidary style of Marcus Aurelius. The style is once again an index to the man.

Yes, I was trying to imitate the style of *Marcus Aurelius to Himself,* and I have failed. Not only because I lack his purity and goodness, but because while he was able to write of the good things he learned from a good family and good friends, I must write of those bitter things I learned from a family of murderers in an age diseased by the quarrels and intolerance of a sect whose purpose it is to overthrow that civilization whose first note was struck upon blind Homer's lyre. I am not Marcus Aurelius, in excellence or in experience.

This is not idle modesty, although Julian may hope that we understand it as that, for the mature Julian genuinely lacks the studied integrity of Marcus Aurelius. In Vidal's imaginative re-creation of him, we are invited to see Julian as a proud and elegant strategist in the battle for power; his study of philosophy and his worship of the gods are not the brave defiance of a last pagan but the maneuvering of a cool, political intelligence. A distinct chill undercuts Julian's appeal as a consequence, his candor and his elevated sentiments notwithstanding.

It is difficult not to be chilled by Julian's claim to love philosophy, because we see so much of his love for military exploit and so little of his love for the examined life. "Multiplicity is the nature of life," Julian may typically declaim, but such a crude, unadorned thesis is only pseudo-philosophy at best. Indeed, Julian amusedly acknowledges his infidelity to philosophical thought on two occasions. Once, when dreaming of surpassing Alexander's conquests, he asks with affected whimsy, "Oh, where is philosophy, now?" When dying, he gently parodies the philosophical wisdom that he might have sought instead of military glory: "Always, in war—no matter what—wear armour," he murmurs, as if it were the achieved wisdom of his life.

In the world of *Julian*, the study of philosophy is a refuge for the unambitious, the untalented, and the unbarbered. Since Julian is neither unambitious nor untalented, we must conclude that he poses ignobly as a student of philosophy, probably to minimize his threat to Constantius. Of his father, who lost his life to Constantius, Julian says significantly, "He was gentle; he was weak; he was destroyed," showing that he knows well that the gentleness of life he affects as a student of philosophy is really a fool's estate. In his quiet, syntactic echoing of the famous inscription displayed in Julius Caesar's Pontic campaign ("I came, I saw, I conquered"), Julian seems actually to mock the gentle life to which his father and Marcus Aurelius stand testament.

Julian's attitude toward Christianity runs deeper in him, of course, than his attitude toward philosophy, and there are many scenes in the novel that establish convincingly his distaste for Christianity and all its works. Yet Priscus is not convinced that the emperor's distaste for Christianity was as religiously motivated as Julian would have insisted:

I suspect the origin of Julian's disaffection is in his family. Constantius was a passionate Christian, absorbed by doctrinal disputes. With good reason, Julian hated Constantius. Therefore, he hated Christianity. This puts the matter far too simply, yet I always tend to the obvious view of things since it is usually the correct one, though of course one can never get to the bottom of anything so mysterious as another man's character, and there is a mystery here.

We tend, like Priscus, to be chilled by the incon-

sistencies of fact and feeling that compromise Julian's
religiosity. Julian always insists that his reestablish-
ment of the old gods was popular with the Army, for
instance, but Priscus says that is "quite untrue,"
merely one of Julian's several self-delusions in matters religious. Julian is inconsistent about his rever-
ence for omens and oracles. He reverences omens
that augur military victory and political success, but
with notable irreverence he opportunely rationalizes
omens that seem to augur ill fortune. When Julian's
shield breaks loose from its handle during a mock
combat session, apparently portending that he will
lose the Gallic provinces, Julian quickly holds up the
handle of the shield before his assembled troops and
proclaims, "I have what I was holding!" channeling
egregiously their interpretation of the omen.

As the oracles turn increasingly against him during the Persian campaign, Julian's attitude is ambiguous and ultimately inconsistent. The Delphic oracle
tells him in unmistakable terms that the gods are
dead and wish to remain so, and Julian can only stand
silent before this blanket rejection of his *raison
d'être*, believing too much in the authenticity of oracles to leap to Priscus's conclusion that the Delphic
priestess was in the pay of the Christians and believing too little in their authenticity to bow before his
fate. Even on his deathbed, disillusioned and bitter,
all his sacrifices to the gods apparently in vain, Julian
cries out equivocally that the gods "raise us up for
sport, and throw us down again," denying the gods
emotionally but not denying them ontologically, not
wholly committed to his religious credo even at the
end.

Another aspect of Julian's religiosity is still more
troubling. As Julian plunges deeply into his fate, and
as the omens and the auguries begin to cast long
shadows over him, we cannot help considering his

increasingly frenzied hecatombs and his anxious searching of the livers of animals the rankest superstition. He seems actually to express in a pagan mode the excesses of sensibility that he denounces in Christianity, for his tortuous ingenuity in scanning the livers of animals is quite as bizarre as the ingenuity of fourth-century Christians in scanning Christ's relationship to the Father. Priscus seems to be making this point when he notes that the emperor had a "craving for the vague and incomprehensible which is essentially Asiatic" and suggests that at heart Julian was "a Christian mystic gone wrong."

It is undoubtedly significant that Julian's apostasy from Christianity is coincident in his own mind with Gallus's elevation to the rank of Caesar. The coincidence suggests that Julian's decision to apostasize is explicable not only as a symbolic rejection of the militant Christians Gallus and Constantius but also as an act of sibling rivalry, the younger brother staking mental territory as his older brother becomes Caesar over all the East. Yet Julian's relationship with Gallus is richer in import than this, as Julian's analysis of their early relationship makes clear.

Gallus and I had each other for company but we were not true brothers in any but the family sense—and only *half*-brothers at that, for we had different mothers. We were like two potentially hostile animals in the same cage. Yet I was ravished by his beauty, and impressed by his energy. Gallus was always doing something which I wanted to imitate. Sometimes he let me, but more often not, for he enjoyed tormenting me. It gave him particular pleasure to quarrel with me just before we were to go hunting. Then he could exclaim, "All right! You stay home. This is a day for men." And the soldiers would laugh at me and I would flee while the exuberant Gallus would ride forth to hunt, as dogs barked and horns sounded through the dark green

woods. But when I was allowed to go with him, I was close
to ecstasy.

This is a truly awesome complex to beleaguer an
adolescent male: enmity without compass to express
itself, incestuous homoerotic desire, looming *rites de
passage*, sibling rejection, adult scorn, and shaming
gratitude. Julian's relationship to Gallus is obviously
fraught with psychic trauma.

We glimpse the trauma of Julian's relationship
with Gallus again in the strange, almost surrealistic
scene in which Julian discovers his brother torturing
Hilarius, Julian's groom. We have a terrible sense of
having stumbled upon Julian's innermost fantasy, for
the groom is as captive and naked as Julian's psyche
before Gallus's inexplicable wrath. Surely Hilarius is
Julian's projection of himself; the sibling relationship
is unresolved and unresolvable in the scene, and Julian's trauma is dramatized superbly. Julian himself
has little insight into the scene and dismisses it as
"curious," but he knows enough of his general relationship with Gallus to realize that his brother has
robbed him in an essential way of his will.

We can hypothesize that Gallus stands to Julian
both as an ideal self and as an anti-self, with Gallus's
vigorous, intolerant manhood the focus of Julian's
passionate admiration and the object of his equally
passionate scorn. This psychic irresolution seems to
be seminal to all that is ambiguous and troubling in
Julian. It explains obliquely, for instance, Julian's sexual prudery, his sudden impulses to exercise a "perfect tyranny," and his Christian mysticism *manqué*.
It explains more directly his overweening determination to succeed in the offices in which Gallus fails.
It explains neatly his failure to project a coherent
persona in his autobiographical writings.

This interpretation of Julian's feeling for Gallus

is only a hypothesis, however. Julian remains deep in the shadows of history; the dynamics governing his character and his career are calculatedly unresolved and only conjectural in our understanding. Priscus's conclusion that "one can never get to the bottom of another man's character" is Vidal's ultimate word on Julian as it was his first word on him in *Messiah;* his distancing effects and the ambivalence of his attitude toward Julian support that fundamental truth. In a significant evolution of Vidal's sensibility, Eugene Luther's discovery that Julian was too remote to be evoked successfully ceased to be Vidal's artistic problem and became his artistic theme.

There is a special artfulness to *Julian*'s irresolution. If *Julian* has not the lucidity of Robert Graves's *I, Claudius* (1934) or Thornton Wilder's *The Ides of March* (1948), historical novels that stand prototypically behind it, neither does it misrepresent the past as a living present, as those novels tend to do. The historical novel is considered a minor art form precisely because temporal sleight of hand is too dominant among its effects. It is both *Julian*'s modesty as a historical novel and its distinction that it allows dust to overlay its use of the present tense, distance to mute its contemporary point of view, and Julian himself to remain pale and enigmatic.

Creation (1981) is a historical novel of more traditional cut than *Julian*. Its central character and narrator is the fictional Cyrus Spitama, an aged diplomat, half Persian and half Ionian Greek, whom Vidal imagines the grandson of the Persian prophet Zoroaster. Cyrus's story begins in the year 445 B.C. when he happens to hear the Greek historian Herodotus discourse on the Persian-Greek wars. He is so outraged by Herodotus's partisan account that he resolves in this last year of his life to set the record straight, and he therefore consents to a nephew's long-standing plea that he record his memoirs. The nephew is Democritus, who would be known to later antiquity as the "Laughing Philosopher," and because Cyrus is blind and infirm, Democritus serves as his amanuensis. "So make yourself comfortable," Cyrus tells his young nephew. "I have a long memory, and I shall indulge it."

Cyrus's memory is long indeed, and his narrative cuts a swath not merely through the Persian-Greek wars but through most of the fifth-century world. He begins with an account of Zoroaster's assassination, which he witnessed at the age of seven, and he subsequently describes his early life at the Persian imperial court, where he and his mother found sanctuary in the harem. In a rambling, anecdotal narrative, he goes on to discuss his almost sixty years of service to the Persian empire, primarily in ambassadorial posts in far-flung corners of the earth.

In his travels, Cyrus has met an extraordinary number of world figures, and much of his narrative consists of exuberant name-dropping. As the Emperor Darius's representative, Cyrus went to India and visited with the Buddha and with Master Li. The Emperor Xerxes sent him to China to open a trade route, and although he was enslaved several times in China, he managed to go fishing with Confucius and to spend long hours at the sage's feet, listening to his discourses. In the last year of his life he is the Emperor Artaxerxes's ambassador to Athens and deals tartly with Anaxagoras and Pericles. He even hires a young man named Socrates to repair (ineptly, as it happens) a masonry wall. Such names as Aeschylus, Sophocles, Protagoras, Pythagoras, and Lao-tse further adorn the text of the memoir, for the fifth century was host to an unusual number of notable men.

Despite all his travels and his open-minded curi-

osity about the variety of religious belief, Cyrus remains Zoroaster's spiritual legatee. His self-con-
ceived destiny—more honored in intention than in
act—is to reconcile his grandfather's monotheism
with the existence of evil, which is the problem of
"creation" as he sees it and the only subject worth
pondering. Thus, he questions the Buddha and Confucius on their thoughts about creation, and the Jains
and the Taoists as well, turning his ambassadorial
missions into something of a philosophical quest.

Answers, however, are not forthcoming. There
is no need to know how things began, the Buddha
assures him, and Confucius has no interest in how the
world was created or for what purpose. The Jains
suggest that he poses a false question, predicated on
an unbeliever's belief in time, and when he asks
Master Li how creation came about, the preacher of
the Tao answers simply, "I do not know whose child
it is." His search for a religious explanation of creation is in vain, and the crowning irony of the novel
is that he relates the story of this quest to Democritus, whom students know today as an important
philosopher of materialism. "Matter is all," Democritus insists in a supercilious addendum to the memoir, his materialism seizing the last word in the novel
as it would seize it in history.

Like *Julian, Creation* is a work of impressive historicity. It is fascinating to read of an ostracism
ceremony in which the Greek citizenry could vote to
exile those who happened to bore them and no less
fascinating to learn of Indian mariners who refused
to serve on Persian ships in the belief that magnetic
rocks would pop the iron nails. We are enchanted by
the aplomb of a Chinese duchess who chose to burn
to death in her palace because there was no one of
sufficient rank to escort her out with seemliness. We
read of Queen Artemisia, who leads her troops in the

battle of Salamis sporting a luxuriant false beard, and of elephants whose tantrums rival those of the harem when their drivers attend to other pachyderms. Gorgeously decadent court ceremonies, winsome temple prostitutes, bazaars the world over—the novel is not only a geographical travelogue but a sociological one, surveying the exotica of four ancient cultures.

Creation is not as historically flawless as *Julian*, however, and nit pickers can discover small errors. Vidal is shaky on the routing of Cyrus's travels, as when he sends his protagonist sailing along the coast of India and up the Indus River to the Gangetic kingdoms, an unlikely route in itself and extraordinarily difficult for ships of the day. Wanderers in the Gobi Desert actually plunge their faces into phantasmagorical water holes and choke on mouthfuls of sand, for Vidal giddily suspends the laws of optics that govern mirages. Jainism was not quite the ancient sect in the fifth century that Vidal represents it as—it was more like a century old. And as Mary Renault points out, the carvers of the Persepolis reliefs would be startled to learn that hands were not uncovered in the presence of the Persian kings.[4] Inasmuch as he is half Greek, Cyrus himself enjoys an unlikely longevity in Persian service during the Persian-Greek wars. His longevity is rendered still more unlikely by his Zoroastrian eminence at a time when the Persian kings found it necessary to play down their official religion.

Nonetheless, *Creation* is well researched in the main; its historicity is so generally impressive that small errors of authenticity seem unimportant. Vidal is particularly adept at illumining the "what ifs" of history. He sets us to wondering, for example, what would have happened if Persia had turned to a conquest of India and China, as his protagonist advises. The Persian defeat at Marathon was as much the consequence of palace intrigue as of the Plataean and

Athenian alliance, Vidal hypothesizes, and he leaves
us to speculate whether the battle of Marathon
would have occurred had Persia deflected her court's
interests eastward. As is his wont, Vidal even deals in
revisionist theory. Herodotus's *History* tells of an im-
postor seizing the throne of Persia on Cambyses's
death, but Vidal has it that Darius invented that story
to justify his overthrow of the alleged imposter, who
was in reality Cambyses's rightful heir.

These "what ifs" energize the novel. Cyrus's divided heritage is a useful ploy, however unlikely it
renders his service to Persia, for it necessitates that
he pay close attention to goings-on at the various
courts. His resultant accounts of the stylized humility
and bald hypocrisy of court life are fabulous stuff in
our antiformalist age. Similarly, Cyrus's mixed heritage enables Vidal to create an enlivening tension
between Greek curiosity and Persian orthodoxy in
Cyrus's point of view. Cyrus believes himself entirely
Persian in point of view, of course, and it is one of the
great pleasures of the novel that his curmudgeonly
stance vis-à-vis the Athenians is therefore reduced to
a tour de force. The cradle of the Western democra-
cies is a parlous place, he tells us with a shudder of
distaste, "because at any moment these volatile people are apt to hold one of their assemblies in which
every male citizen may speak his mind and, worst of
all, vote." The Athenians' vaunted temples are vulgar imitations of Persian architecture, he maintains
with iconoclastic verve, and he insists that the
Athenians are a universally impious people despite
an entire readiness to accuse their enemies of impiety. "And if you happen to be unpopular that week,"
Cyrus adds contemptuously, "you can be con-
demned to death." Fickle and easily bored, the
founders of democracy have no taste for political sta-

bility, he says. "In their eyes, nothing old can be good, while nothing new can be bad—until it is old."

The joke, of course, is that Cyrus fails to appreciate the magnitude of his own taste for change. He fails also to recognize the creeping impiety that leads him to question Zoroaster's teachings, especially as he discovers Zoroaster's borrowings from older religions and begins to see the resemblance between Indian vedas and sacred Persian stories. Cyrus's old-age blindness is an effective symbol of his refusal to face this radical dividedness in his point of view, for the blindness comes over him one day while he is looking in a mirror.

Creation is distinguished by abundant invention as well as by historicity, but like many of Vidal's novels it gives short measure on plot. Cyrus's physical journeys and his search for religious answers provide a framework for the novel, but the myriad details of his odyssey tend to assert an immediate interest, independent of the framework. The novel seems in consequence not so much a narrative as a gallery hung with several serious portraits, a number of caricatures, and a great many genre studies, with almost all of the hangings superior to the overarching gallery itself.

The portraits are *Creation*'s distinction. One of the most vivid portraits is that of Gosala, a maverick Jain who claims to be near the end of 84,000 rebirths and whose notion that each of us must endure that full cycle of rebirths chills Cyrus to the bone. The Buddha, on the other hand, is a strange, enigmatic figure, and Cyrus finds his dispassion and empty amusement with all things human not only chilling but frightening. One of the most appealing portraits in the novel is that of Ambalika, Cyrus's Indian wife, who adjusts to her politically arranged marriage with practical good sense, her sixty-four wifely arts tidily ordered, her sense of her wifely due impeccable. The portrait of Prince Jeta, Ambalika's grandfather, is perhaps the most delicate in Vidal's gallery. An elegant, worldly aesthete, he is a paradigm of mannerliness but with such good sense and tact withal that his mannerliness seems kindness; his formality, candor. Vidal sketches this elusive synthesis with an artful economy of line:

Prince Jeta greeted us formally. He told me how delighted he was that I was marrying his granddaughter, who was, everyone agreed, as light-footed as a gazelle, as fertile as fresh lettuce, and so on. I was pleased that he did not pretend to know the child.

But the portrait of Confucius is the centerpiece of Vidal's gallery. The author's genius is to render the Chinese sage as both a large-minded mystic and (with some historical basis) a small-minded politico. Lusting for civil power, he has to fall back continually upon philosophy, as upon an uncomfortable, worn-out mattress, and he wears out the pages of his *I Ching*, Vidal tells us, no more rapidly than he wears out the patience of Chinese authorities. A sardonic temperament renders Confucius grittily human. Rather bored with his own mystique, he is capable of mocking Cyrus's excessive deference:

I was startled to find how often this traditionalist sage was at odds with received opinion. For instance, when I asked him what the latest tortoise-shell auguries had foretold, he said, "The shell asked to be reunited with the tortoise."
    "Is that a proverb, Master?"
    "No, honored guest, a joke."

In a novel crammed with pretentious and posturing characters, Confucius also stands out because his knowledge of his predicament is entirely lucid.

But Confucius seemed not to take himself for granted in

quite the same way that most eminent men do. "What I am considered to be and what I am are two different things. Like the fish, which is one thing in the water and another on the plate. I am a teacher because no one will allow me to conduct the affairs of a state. I'm like the bitter gourd: they hang me on the wall as a decoration, but I am not used."

This is verisimilitude *al dente,* firm and toothsome. However, such passages set a standard to which the rest of the novel does not often rise. Indeed, for all its fascinating historicity, *Creation* too often fails to achieve an adequate level of verisimilitude. The *mise-en-scène* is too obvious, the meetings with notables too inexorable. One longs to have Cyrus sit at campfires as well as at the feet of kings and sages, scratching his beard and worrying about strange noises in the night. "I have no intention of revealing to the Greeks *any* details of my journey to Cathay," Cyrus says typically, and such remarks are the excuse for an equally typical elision in the narrative; the author is less concerned with rendering the weariness and anxieties of Cyrus's journeys than with moving him expeditiously to the next celebrity. At such moments the historicity of the novel seems unfleshed, as dry and distanced a historicity as *Julian*'s but without *Julian*'s fine patina to justify the dust of time.

At other moments, however, it seems as if an unwritten and much darker text lay hidden within *Creation*'s amplitude, for aphoristic nuggets of political wisdom adorn the text in the same way that the portraits adorn it. In concert, these nuggets suggest that *Creation* might have been a handbook of courtly politics, *à la* Machiavelli, had Cyrus suffered less from an old man's logorrhea. "Hereditary priests usually tend to atheism," Cyrus warns us. Why? "They know too much." On court patronage, he is

succinct: "One is promised everything; then given
nothing." "Protocol was particularly strict at the
court of Darius," he notes drily, "as it tends to be
whenever a monarch is not born to the throne." On
lying: "Zoroaster would have approved of my perfect
insincerity. He always said that we live in a world not
of our own making." On princely empathy: "The
half-smile was now a full smile. The tragedy of others
has that effect on princes."

Vidal's sentences, of course, glimmer through
any amount of dust and through the most overbear-
ing and unnecessary amplitude. Classically graceful,
totally poised, and brimming with quiet intelligence,
they are the masterstrokes in all his fictions. Cyrus
has the gift of Vidal's narrators for just such marvelous sentences. "All things turn out ill, in the end. But
that is the ill nature of things, to end." "I was fearless.
I was stupid. I was young." "At the beginning Xerxes
understood men; and their vanity." "For the Greek,
what is not Greek is not." Cyrus's summation of his
years in India and Cathay is as fine a passage, perhaps, as Vidal has ever wrought.

When I think of India, gold flares in the darkness behind
the lids of these blind eyes. When I think of Cathay, silver
gleams and I see again, as if I were really seeing, silver
snow fall against silver willows.

Gold and silver; darkness now.

The aesthetic success of *Creation* rests not with
its large story but with such silver-and-gold moments.

5

The American Trilogy:
Washington, D.C., Burr, 1876

Vidal has maintained a serious interest in American politics almost his entire life. He is not only a pundit who haunts television talk shows in election years and an *arbiter elegantarium* of political behavior but also an occasional participant in the political fray. He campaigned actively for Senator Eugene McCarthy in McCarthy's presidential bid of 1968, and he has been active from time to time in movements to launch a new political party; he was a congressional candidate in 1960, and since 1975 he has issued several "State of the Union" addresses designed to show up the presidential address. The Presidency, Vidal once remarked whimsically, is the only thing he ever wanted that he has not achieved,[1] but he is almost certainly less whimsical about such political ambitions than he wants us to believe. It is no surprise that a substantial portion of Vidal's writing has taken American politics as its subject, most notably the trilogy composed of *Washington, D.C., Burr,* and *1876.*[2]

Washington, D.C. (1967) begins on July 22, 1937, at a party celebrating the defeat of President Roosevelt's attempt to enlarge the Supreme Court, and it proceeds against a backdrop of just such momentous

events—Pearl Harbor, Roosevelt's death, the
McCarthy investigations, and Korea—each following
in its turn. The novel focuses on two families. One
family consists of James Burden Day, an influential
senator from an unnamed state in America's heart-
land, his wife Kitty, and their daughter Diana; the
other family consists of Blaise Sanford, the owner of
the *Washington Tribune*, his wife Frederika, and
their children, Enid and Peter. Clay Overbury, Senator Day's protégé, links the two families when he
marries Enid Sanford, and the novel charts Clay's
unscrupulous rise to power, first through the influence he gains over Blaise Sanford as he displaces
Enid in her father's affections and then through his
blackmailing of Senator Day, who had once accepted
a bribe.

Structurally, Clay is at the novel's center, but he
is as moribund as his name implies, and Senator Day
is the novel's one character of substance and vitality.
As Vidal himself has pointed out, the senator faces a
thoroughly realistic dilemma when he must decide
whether to accept the bribe that is his undoing, for
he feels a moral obligation to save the republic from
FDR by winning the Presidency himself, yet he cannot finance a presidential campaign without violat-
ing his moral sense and accepting the bribe.[3]
Ultimately, Day is driven to suicide by the prospect
of exposure, and the novel closes with a party scene
that mirrors the novel's opening, with the significant
difference that a door which had been opened upon
Clay in the first pages is now firmly locked. The range
of political possibility in America is diminished with
Senator Day's death, we understand, and the republic's store of idealism is less than it was.

Considered simply as a political novel, *Washington, D.C.* delivers a number of shrewd insights. Senator Day remarks to young Peter Sanford that of all

the lives he can think of, political life is the most humiliating, and his remark is much more than characterization. In some ways, the remark is Vidal's most fundamental comment on what the American system does to its statesmen. Similarly, Senator Day is not merely sloganizing when he remarks to his daughter that timeserving is the secret of survival in politics; he is, rather, enunciating a political truth as deeply embedded in the novel's plot as in the national history. Again, a passage about the senatorial "Club" offers a glimpse into the corridors of power, impressive in its reductionism and authority:

No one was ever quite sure who belonged to The Club since members denied its existence but everyone knew who did not belong. The club was permanently closed to the outsize personality, to the firebrand tribune of the people, to the Senator running too crudely for President. Members of The Club preferred to do their work quietly and to get re-elected without fanfare. On principle they detested the President, and despite that magnate's power to loose and to bind, The Club ruled the Senate in its own way and for its own ends, usually contrary to those of the President.

The novel is particularly rich in contemporary insights, especially the seamier side of political life in the 1940s. "Like so many of the American magnates," we are told of Blaise Sanford, he "vacillated between despair at Hitler's continuing success and terror that Hitler might fail in Russia." With kindred acerbity, Vidal mocks in another key the WASP pretense of the 1940s that FDR was Jewish, for that is surely the purpose of Frederika Sanford's lunatic insistence that the British royal family is Jewish. Commemorating the same tradition of WASP invective, Peter Sanford opines that Irish-Americans tend to regard the demagogic Senator McCarthy "as chosen by God to shield them from civilization." In still another key, allusions to the herding of Japanese citizens into concentration camps on the West Coast evoke the high-handedness of the wartime government, while Clay's admiration for Roosevelt's imperialism commemorates the attractions of empire for many Americans in the postwar decade.

Such censorious evocations are rarely the stuff of history books, of course, for they are based on intuitive insights and are deeply partisan. They are the mother wit of one who was there rather than the dispassionate conclusions of a scholar, and in a sense they are more like gossip than history. Yet as Peter Sanford reflects, "History is gossip . . . the trick was in determining which gossip is history." Like Saint-Simon at the court of Louis XIV, Vidal transforms gossip into history, and his view of this period in American history is both significant and absorbing.

But *Washington, D.C.* is giddily melodramatic at the same time that it is soberly historical. Senator Day is haunted by the specter of his father, who appears to him several times in a bloodied Civil War uniform and calls down imprecations upon the son who sentimentalizes the Civil War while serving in the federal government. The senator identifies with his dead father, of course, in the classic manner of rejected sons, and this identification is complicated by the senator's further identification with Clay, who is both a surrogate son he wishes to treat better than his ghostly father treats him and an alter ego through whom he attempts to replay his sonship more successfully. Symptomatic of this ripe Freudianism is the scene at Bull Run in which the senator's father appears to him, unrecognized, as a young soldier very like Clay. Symptomatic, too, is the scene in which Clay tells the senator that he is joining the Army, for the senator immediately feels the bullet that hit his father at the battle of Shiloh tear through his own shoulder. The senator's suicide, rendered as a final confrontation with his father, is nakedly Gothic and quite wonderful of its kind.

With stiff fingers Burden removed a handkerchief from his pocket. Then he walked toward the wounded soldier, half expecting him to run away. But this was no ordinary youth; it was his father honorably struck by an enemy's bullet in the field of battle. The Confederate corporal did not flinch even when at last they were face to face.

For a long moment Burden stared into the blue eyes that perfectly reflected empty sky. Then slowly he extended the hand which held the handkerchief. Now only the rifle barred his way. He waited patiently until at last, marvelously, the rifle was lowered. With a cry he flung himself upon the youth who was his father, plunged the handkerchief into the wound, lost his balance, fell against the beloved, was taken into those long-dead arms, and like impatient lovers, they embraced and together fell.

There are many scenes in the novel as melodramatically extravagant and as highly colored as these, although they are usually of a more humorous cast. One thinks of the scene in a hotel dining room in which Senator Day's son-in-law defines liberalism, complete with images of barricades in the streets and the proletariat taking their bread at gunpoint. "Meanwhile the businessmen at the next table fled," we are told, "no doubt to report to the House Un-American Activities Committee that the enemy had seized the dining room of the Willard Hotel." The career of Millicent Smith Carhart, a Washington hostess and the niece of a shadowy President, is melodrama become camp; it is worthy of Oscar Wilde.

Lacking conventional good looks, she had resolutely made herself interesting by, among other things, marrying a British peer. Unfortunately, her belted earl, as she called him, was addicted to *le vice anglais*, and though this might have interested Millicent, it did not please her. Finally, after an otherwise uninteresting dinner party at the American Embassy, she had, in her own phrase, belted the earl. She then returned to Washington, and built a palace on Dupont Circle with the fortune left her by the President, who had died unexpectedly rich. Millicent lived alone until the earl died when, to everyone's surprise, she married Daniel Truscott Carhart, a dim New Englander who interested no one but Millicent. Speculation as to just *how* he interested her continued for many years.

Such passages tend to color the straightforwardly melodramatic elements in the novel: the conspiracy of Clay and Blaise Sanford to commit Enid to an insane asylum, for instance, and Enid's subsequent attempt to kill Blaise, and the suspicion of homosexuality in the relationship between Clay and Blaise. One tends, in consequence, to view each element as seriocomically lurid.

Peter Sanford is the key to the complexity of tone in the novel that results from this interaction of history, melodrama, and humor, and Peter is in many ways Vidal's spokesman, his vehicle for the savoring of *lèse majesté*. Politics both delights and enrages Peter, we are told, as it obviously delights and enrages Vidal, and the characters in the novel seem to Peter to be part of a vast novel in progress, further identifying Peter's stance as auctorial. Indeed, Vidal has allowed Peter to resemble himself in several important ways. By Vidal's own admission, Peter's home is modeled on Merrywood, the Auchincloss estate on the Potomac where Vidal lived when he was Peter's age;[4] Peter also shares Vidal's youthful passion for the cinema, and he even shares Vidal's tendency to gain weight. With almost indelicate intimacy, the death of Peter's friend Scotty echoes the death of James Truscott, Vidal's fellow student at St.

Alban's, just as Bob Ford echoes Truscott so intimately in *The City and the Pillar*.[5]

More specifically, Peter is the key to the novel's tone in that he embodies the conjunction of history, melodrama, and humor. He spends a good deal of time in the Library of Congress studying the career of Aaron Burr, for instance. He is discovered reading Walter Map, the twelfth-century historian and author of *De Nugis Curialium*, and he is discovered reading *The Federalist Papers*. He is gratified to find in Burden Day his ideal of the classic Roman senator, and in later years he is able to point out that Senator Day's favorite quotation from Plato is a forgery. Peter is a student of history, and he brings a consciousness of history to his observations.

Peter is also a student of melodrama, however, and he relishes the discovery of Gothic possibilities in the Washington *mise-en-scène*. In the opening pages of the novel, he is pleasurably excited by the prospect of being struck by lightning, and his theatrically defiant scream to the heavens is entirely typical of him. Having read Poe the winter before, he finds himself consumed with incestuous passion for his sister Enid, and when he is stimulated by the zippers in women's clothing and can think of nothing but rape, he fancies himself Poe-esquely mad. The violent antipathy between Clay and Blaise in the early months of their association gratifies Peter's taste for raw passion; if the alliance that later develops between the two men disappoints him, he thrills to the promise of "rich drama" when Clay and Blaise must deal with Enid.

But Peter is not self-deluded. The novel may open with Peter standing in a storm-lashed garden, playing at King Lear and daring the lightning to strike him, but Peter knows playacting for what it is, and so he strolls to a lavatory, where he repeats his

cry of defiance before a mirror so that he can watch
the veins knot in his temples. Indeed, that is Peter's
distinction in the novel; he knows his predilection for
melodrama as other characters in the novel do not.
Thus, he can never take seriously Enid's notion that
Blaise is in love with Clay or, on the other hand, think
badly of himself simply because his father rejects
him. Neither can he bestir himself very much about
the incestuous feelings that he cultivates for Enid.
He is neither Senator Day, the victim of an overac-
tive sense of melodrama, nor Clay, so totally lacking
in the melodramatic imagination as never to taste its
joys. The melodrama of both familial and political life
is a matter of choosing to see the melodrama, Peter
knows; if he chooses to see life as a melodrama, it is
simply because life is more amusing when it is highly
colored.

Peter's fondness for all things Hollywood imparts a special edge to the melodramatics of *Washington, D.C.*, for American politics and Hollywood
scenarios merge so often in Peter's mind as to suggest
that the national life takes its keynote from Hollywood. Upon hearing the news of Pearl Harbor and
realizing that America's entrance into the war is imminent, Peter immediately envisions a newsreel,
complete with background music and a narrator's
grave voice announcing, "Heroism took on a new
meaning when Peter Sanford, alone, unaided,
stormed an enemy position. . . ." Connections between Hollywood and the national life are unmistak-
ably limned: Clay Overbury rises to political
eminence through something very like the Hollywood star system (there are dark hints of a casting
couch), and the merchandising of Clay is patterned
on Hollywood's promotional methods. Harold
Griffiths, who is effectively Clay's press agent, is even

a sometime film critic who believes that movies are life "with the point made simple."

But it is once again Peter's distinction in the novel that he knows where Hollywood ends and reality begins. He finds it distasteful that a famous movie star actually *votes*, and when he learns that Scotty has been killed in action, he resents the newsreels that play melodramatically in his head, preferring to rise to tragedy or sink to grief. When Enid dies, on the other hand, Peter tries desperately and without success to imagine an innocuous, Hollywood-style revision of the scenario recounted by her attending doctor. Characteristically, however, his grasp of reality is firm.

It is wholly fitting, then, that Peter is the only character in the novel whose success is not tawdry. Through his involvement with a journal of opinion, he arranges that his father and Clay Overbury do not win easily, and he thereby avenges Enid; through his involvement with the egregious Irene Bloch and her introduction into Laurel House, he strikes a blow against WASP complacency; and through his involvement with Diana, he achieves the only relationship in the novel that is remotely honest and healthy. Yet like Senator Day, Peter is an off-center presence in the novel, and his relative success is a minor irony, just as Senator Day's relative integrity is a sidelined hope. Clay Overbury's climb to a shabby eminence remains the central thread of the novel, and the republic's taste for melodrama remains the novel's trenchant theme. In the last analysis, *Washington, D.C.* is a comedy of political manners.

Burr (1973) is set in the 1830s and is narrated by Charlie Schuyler, a young law clerk with journalistic ambitions who is employed and befriended by Aaron Burr. Burr is a New York City lawyer of advanced

years in the 1830s, but he is still notorious as the man
who killed Alexander Hamilton in a duel in 1804 and
as the author of a secessionist conspiracy in 1806.
Burr is, in fact, so notorious that Charlie is secretly
hired to discredit Vice-President Martin Van Buren
by writing a pamphlet asserting that Van Buren is
Burr's bastard son. Charlie's consequent probing of
Burr's life encourages Burr to reminisce and to hand
over to Charlie his written account of the early days
of the republic. Charlie incorporates Burr's account
of those days into the narrative, alternating great
gobs of Burr's material with his own. Indeed, Charlie's probing of Burr's fatherhood is less significant for
what it finally uncovers—that he and Van Buren are
both Burr's sons—than for its analogue in Burr's
probing of the Founding Fathers.

The giants of the early republic are no heroes to
Burr, and he paints compelling, gossipy portraits.
George Washington was a man of "eerie incompetence" and a backside threatening always to split his
trousers; the Marquis de Lafayette was all silliness
and a pointed head; Alexander Hamilton was a social-
climbing West Indian who read women's novels on
the sly; John Hancock went to his grave piqued that
Washington and not he had commanded the Continental Army; Thomas Jefferson was a hypocrite who
pledged his countrymen's lives but never his own. In
Burr's view, the Founding Fathers were so many
despoilers of the infant republic. He sees Washington
as building a strong central government simply to
protect his land holdings, and he sees Jefferson as
amassing a Napoleonic empire and trampling on civil
liberties in the process. Having thought the Constitution too brittle a document to last even fifty years,
Burr nevertheless affects to be scandalized that those
who had framed the Constitution subverted it so

casually, and his accounts of their political wrangles are as damning and fascinating as they are ample.

But Burr has axes to grind, it is clear, and much of the material he gives Charlie is self-justifying and emphasizes his own good sense and refinement. He is, he admits, something of a rake, but an elegant, Augustan rake and a patrician scoundrel to the degree that he is a scoundrel at all. Charlie tends to think the old reprobate beyond criticism, yet Charlie's sections of the novel make clear that Burr is still an unregenerate adventurer, as exemplified by his marriage to the wealthy ex-prostitute Madame Jumel and his loss of her money in a Texas land-lease fraud. The novel is, in fact, nothing so much as a composite portrait of Aaron Burr—disjointed, fictionalized, and honorific, to be sure, part biography and part autobiography *manqué*, but a portrait of Burr nonetheless.

The portrait is untenable, of course, to the degree that it is partisan and omits elements of Burr's life recorded elsewhere. There is no mention of Burr's having been raised until he was thirteen in the home of a brutal, bachelor uncle, presumably because such mention would make too predictable his maverick impulses and notorious womanizing. And the very odd relationship between Burr and his daughter Theodosia—a Freudian set piece if there ever was one—seems to exist at face value, just as Burr's insistence that he never wanted to be emperor of the American West (merely emperor of Mexico) seems to prevail, although Henry Adams and the majority of historians believe that Burr did attempt to separate the Western territories from the union, exactly as Jefferson charged. Yet these suppressions and misrepresentations are portraiture, too, for they are part of Burr's carefully prepared brief for himself and wholly consonant with his opportunism.

The portraits of the Founding Fathers are similarly shaded. Jefferson was certainly a duplicitous man, as Burr charges, and he certainly took up the cause of states' rights in order to gain votes; he was even the compulsive explainer of the obvious that Burr ridicules. But with equal certainty, it is a shaded viewpoint that sees Jefferson as no more than that, just as it is a shaded viewpoint that Washington endorsed a strong central government simply to protect Mount Vernon, for hundreds of other landowners bitterly opposed the formation of a strong central government. In short, Burr and his author are all too ready to see the ambitions of these men and too little ready to see the men. A historian might object they are too ready to see the men and too little ready to see the historical forces that shaped them.

But who would have it otherwise? Shading imparts depth and texture to a narrative as much as to a photograph or painting, and *Burr* is absorbing precisely because it debunks the Founding Fathers so gloriously. Burr remarks of Washington, for instance, that "the fine white powder he used to dress his hair sometimes gave the startling effect of a cloudy nimbus about that storied head." One has only to think of the halo effect in so many of Washington's portraits to catch Vidal's superb iconoclasm, meshed so artfully with the period detail. Similarly, when Burr visits Jefferson's rented home at Gray's Ferry, he is treated to a demonstration of a bed that rises to the ceiling on ropes (a duplicate of the famous Jefferson gadget that draws tourists to Monticello today), and Burr's simple bewilderment as to why anyone would *wish* to send his bed to the ceiling is a neat deflation of Archimedes redux. It does not harm the fun that the bed crashes to the floor when the ropes break, "nearly sparing us the Jefferson administration." Just as one must admire Vidal's restraint in not making overt the connection between Washington's hair powder and his portraits, so one must admire his restraint in not connecting Jefferson's ludicrous copying machines—a repeating joke in every sense —with the many replications of Jefferson among the slave children at Monticello or with Jefferson's astonishing ability to stand on both sides of every question. Doubleness is in a sense Jefferson's keynote in the novel, but Burr and his author have too much respect for the debunking stance to resort to overkill.

Indeed, Burr and his author are wonderfully adept at the casual remark that debunks gratuitously. The Virginians' dominance of the country's political machinery inspires Burr not to a focused peroration but to an incidental remark about "the many-limbed Virginian junto, the octopus with but a single Jeffersonian head and a thousand tentacles, all named James!" The invidious word "junto" cuts the Virginians sharply to size, the octopus conceit is nicely rude, and the allusion to a proliferation of Jameses in political life is lightly parodic. This descending scale of invective softens the harshness of "junto" without for a moment mitigating its sting, and it is highly effective rhetoric.

Similarly, the early republic's lust for empire is debunked much more successfully in the small scene than in the large plot. The preposterous Madame Jumel (otherwise known as Eliza Bowen of Rhode Island) shifts between New England Yankee and emigré French in her accent, and she evokes in miniature the American fascination with Bonaparte and the French empire in the 1780s. If her devotion to the emperor is absurdly pretentious, it is the exact equivalent of Jefferson's ambition to match Bonaparte empire for empire. Only Burr and his author are sufficiently patrician to snub the Corsican: Bonaparte was apparently too great a man to notice

weather, Burr remarks with studied indirection, for
he failed to understand that autumn is invariably
followed by winter and that in Russia winter is invin-
cible. Alluding to the influence of Empire fashion on
American clothing, Burr remarks simply and contemptuously that the summer of 1807 was one of
"teats and treason."

There is almost no aspect of American life between 1776 and 1830 that is not debunked in this
incidental manner. The government is blatantly anti-
Catholic, Burr assures us in an aside, and he himself
finds it impossible to believe that a Catholic can be
a good American. The Continental Army may have
suffered at Valley Forge, but our attention is casually
drawn to the nation's founders spending the winter
quite comfortably before their fires. Burr remarks
that bad manners in America began with the French
Revolution—that overnight it became slavish for the
lower classes to be polite to anyone—and Charlie
maintains, without especial point, that Washington
Irving goes to the opposite extreme of conduct and
threatens to suffocate one and all with his "constant
benevolent blandness." Ambassadorships are eagerly
sought, we learn, because they take people out of
America to more civilized lands. Martha Washington
has a "disquieting tendency to nod or shake her head
for no particular reason," Burr tells us, apropos of
nothing. The colonists did not win the Revolutionary
War, he claims; rather, the French won it for them.
Slavery is not really one of Burr's concerns, yet Jeffersonian democracy, he suggests, is a matter of "honest
yeomen enjoying the fruits of black labor."

One of Vidal's more delightful creations in this
vein is Mrs. Townsend, who presides over a brothel
that Burr and Charlie frequent and who is an historically authentic person. Early in the novel, she is discovered reading *Pilgrim's Progress* in a search for the

meaning of life; paralleling the history of American religious sentiment in the eighteenth and nineteenth centuries, she progresses later in the novel to Jonathan Edwards, whom she reads, she says, "for the terror!" An Emersonian interest in Oriental religions later soothes her spirits.

America is a compound of pretension, arrogance, and silliness, then, and the narrator, Charlie Schuyler, finds Burr a refreshing antidote to the tone of the day. Indeed, this is a secret of Burr's immense appeal in the novel for us as well as for Charlie. He pretends to be no more than an opportunist, quite willing to trade his charm for a steady income and the heady delights of power. It gives one pause to realize that unlike the other Fathers (Hamilton is the only exception), Burr never spoke of a national purpose and apparently never even imagined that such an exalted thing could be.

Vidal has caught this aspect of the historical Burr well, and the debunking tone of the novel is perfectly calculated to flatter Burr's lack of cant. Yet Burr is no unimaginative literalist. Charlie notes that he is able to make a trip to his barber sound like a conspiracy to overthrow the government, and his grandiose schemes for the Western territories are certainly imaginative enough, even foolhardy. His marriage to Madame Jumel is no less imaginative. Andrew Jackson was of the opinion that the historical Burr was no fool but as easily fooled as any other man, and Vidal has caught this paradoxical aspect of the historical Burr, too, not shying from depicting him as the dupe of his own ambitions. This is actually part of Vidal's vindication of Burr, for the other Founding Fathers escape the consequences of their ambition all too easily, and the ordinary citizen pays the cost in their stead. Burr is an overreacher as much as they, but he

pays the cost of overreaching with hard cash and
with his permanent reputation.

Burr's charm is essentially verbal, however, and
he is especially a master of the set piece that begins
in arrogance and fades into self-mockery. His reaction to the death of Lafayette is a hoary set piece,
perhaps, but the technique of the abrupt reversal has
never been more elegantly rendered.

[Burr:] "One cannot say that he was taken before his time.
We must restrain our grief." The Colonel was suitably dry.
"He must have been—what, eighty?"
[Sam Swartout:] "Seventy-seven. Younger than you, Colonel."
[Burr:] "Then I shudder at this cold premonitory wind
from France. Poor boy! So much to look forward to. I trust
he is now in Heaven with General Washington and, side by
side, they rest on a cloudy mantle of stars for all eternity,
dreaming up disastrous military engagements."

The elegance of Burr's wit seldom falters. He
remarks of his mother that she died before they
could properly meet, and on being told to his surprise that the poet William Cullen Bryant was once
a Burrite, he remarks, "I shall now read him with a
warmth which hitherto has been lacking." Of his im-
pending death, he says to Charlie, "If you should hear
that I have died in the bosom of the Dutch Reformed
Church, you will know that either a noble mind was
entirely overturned at the end or a man of the cloth
has committed perjury."

This verbal elegance is also part of Burr's vindication, perhaps the most important part. Vidal's
characters are always worthy of respect to the degree that they are fluent, and only Myra Breckinridge can match Burr's high verbal style. Vidal's
equation is not trivial. Sophistication, intellect, and
breeding do manifest themselves in language, and

for Vidal language is the preeminent clue to the man. Burr is superior to the other Founding Fathers whatever the facts of history, then, not simply because he speaks more elegantly than they but because his language is a manifestation of superior being. The Fathers of lesser being are betrayed by their speech. Words always failed Washington, we are assured, for he was utterly incapable of organizing a sentence containing a new thought; Jefferson's self-delusion was echoed in his "tangled sentences and lunatic metaphors," his modest intellect in his inability to achieve irony, wit, or humor.

Charlie Schuyler is a neat foil to Burr, for he is an apprentice *littérateur,* enormously impressed by Burr's gifts and terribly conscious of his own amateurism. He complains at the very beginning of the novel that he is unable to catch the "right tone" in preparing a story about Burr's wedding to Madame Jumel for the *Evening Post,* and he is endearingly self-conscious about his more literary effects, reminding himself to include descriptive detail, pointing out his parody of Washington Irving's style lest we miss it, and assiduously cultivating the "slanderous manner" for his pamphlet on Van Buren and Burr. His respect for language and for verbal style functions as a continuing tribute to Burr, underscoring this important element of Burr's vindication.

But Charlie is an echo of his father as well as a foil. His delight in tricking Burr is something Burr would readily understand, and his fascination with the past and his attraction to what is secret are surely dispositions inherited from Burr. Financial security eludes him just as it eludes his father, and his living with the prostitute Helen Jewett and his false arrest for her murder (the murder of the historical Helen Jewett was a celebrated *crime passionel* of the 1830s) parallel Burr's marriage to the former prostitute Madame Jumel and the legal squabble that ensued.

Charlie does not realize until the last page of the novel that Burr is his natural father, yet he has been looking unconsciously for a father throughout the novel, inasmuch as he is drawn to older men and finds discipleship a congenial role. "I am always obedient," he says. Moreover, he is estranged from his adoptive father, whom he credits with killing his mother three years before the novel opens. In the one scene in which Charlie accidentally meets his adoptive father, he significantly protests almost at once that he must leave to meet Burr. Burr is his chosen father, we understand, even his fairy godfather, for in the last line of the novel Charlie says that "there was no wish that I could make that I have not already been granted by my father Aaron Burr." It is Charlie's miraculous luck that his chosen father is his real father.

As I have already observed, *Burr* is a novel more impressive in the small scene than in the large plot, but this search for a father that constitutes the large plot of the novel contributes nicely to Vidal's large point that America has misunderstood its paternity. Aaron Burr would figure more prominently in the pantheon of the Fathers if history were rightly understood, Vidal seems to say, and the politicos of *Washington, D.C.* might be more impressive men had America adopted the high style of Burr rather than the low style of his coevals. Yet Burr's influence is not dead. Peter Townsend carries on Burr's iconoclasm in *Washington, D.C.*, the chronologically last novel in Vidal's trilogy, and Peter is a stepfamily descendent of Burr, just as Vidal himself is loosely related to Burr through his stepfather, Hugh D. Auchincloss. But Peter Townsend's sniping at the national life from the sidelines of a political journal

is a pale shadow of Burr's fine outsiderhood, just as
Charlie's attack on Burr in his pamphlet is only a
shadow of Burr's debunking of the Founding Fathers
in his memoirs. *"Le style, c'est l'homme,"* according
to the French aphorism, and Vidal would surely
agree. But for Vidal, political style is also passé.

1876 (1976) opens in December 1875, on the eve
of the American centennial year. Charles Schuyler,
the narrator of *Burr,* is sixty-two years old and returns to New York from France for the first time
since 1837. His widowed daughter Emma, the Princess d'Agrigente, accompanies him, and they come
as desperate fortune hunters, since Schuyler has lost
most of his capital in the Panic of 1873 and cannot
support them on his meager earnings as a writer.
1876 is a scribbled journal that Schuyler keeps from
his arrival in New York until his death in the early
months of 1877; he thinks of it as his workbook, a
place to note incidents and impressions that he may
someday write about, a "quarry" from which he
hopes to "hack out a monument or two to decorate
the republic's centennial."

The quarry is ample, for the America of 1876 is
very different from the land Schuyler left almost
forty years before, and he confesses himself unpre-
pared for "the opulence, the grandeur, the vulgarity,
the poverty, the elegance, the awful crowded abundance" that are everywhere, especially in New York
City. Daunted but economically desperate, he
plunges into New York society with Emma on his
arm, and in short order he declares himself a support-
er of Samuel J. Tilden, the Democratic nominee for
President, in the hope that Tilden will appoint him
Minister to France in return for his writing a campaign biography. Schuyler also signs on as a special
correspondent for the New York *Herald,* and his du-

ties take him to cities as far flung as Albany, Cincin-
nati, and Washington. He covers the opening of the
Philadelphia Centennial Exposition, he is a guest at
the Astor estate in Rhinebeck, and he attends the
Republican nominating convention in the Midwest.
In rather too much detail, he traces the collapse of
the Grant administration under the weight of the
Belknap scandal and traces the bitterly contested
Hayes-Tilden presidential election, in which Repub-
licans maneuvered the election into the Electoral
College and stole the Presidency from Tilden, who
had won the popular vote.

In a parallel upset, Schuyler's daughter Emma
breaks her engagement to the scion of a respectable
New York family and marries the flashy millionaire
William Sanford, the grandfather of Peter Sanford of
Washington, D.C. Their marriage is clouded by the
probability that Emma helped Sanford do away with
his former wife, just as the presidential election is
clouded by charges of malfeasance. Aghast, Schuyler
dies shortly afterward while working on the notes
that constitute *1876,* and William Cullen Bryant provides a short obituary in an addendum to the text.

Like the other novels in Vidal's American trilogy, *1876* is meticulously historical and something of
a Cook's Tour, replete with allusions to the thousand
churches of Brooklyn, to goats trotting down East
Twenty-fourth Street, and to the beginnings of
Chinatown in lower Manhattan. But Schuyler is not
the average tour guide, and historical trappings ac-
quire an interesting edge when they are filtered
through his Europeanized mind. The newly completed Central Park raises for him the very European
question, "How does one 'complete' a park?" and his
acquired distaste for Americanisms makes him ask
whether shops are always called "stores" in New
York. Oakey Hall, a former mayor of New York, is the

best dressed man in the city, he reports, "(whatever *that* must be)." The Hudson River estates built in the Gothic style make him grateful that there is no Gothic revival in France—just the Gothic itself—and nineteenth-century landmarks beloved in the twentieth century are especially singled out for his censure. The houses of Washington Square are "as unimaginative as a row of new American novels," he says, and Gramercy Park seems to him a "homely little square . . . surrounded by a perfunctory ironwork fence and the usual narrow houses sprayed with chocolate." Folkways inspire a similar censure: "What'll it be?" is the "gracious question" put to him in a restaurant, and "Welcome home, traitor" is America's inevitable greeting to her expatriates. Titles are alleged to have no place in a democracy, yet he finds that they are shamelessly affected.

Americans care desperately for titles, for any sign of distinction. In fact, since the War Between the States, I have not met a single American of a certain age who does not insist upon being addressed as Colonel or Commodore. Invariably I promote them; address them as General, as Admiral; they preen and do not correct me.

American *littérateurs* are beyond the pale. Mark Twain is "the most contemptible music-hall performer that ever pandered to an audience of ignorant yahoos," and Nathaniel Hawthorne is "that dark veiled lady of New England letters . . . who, faced with *any* truth about the way we are, swiftly evokes ghosts and haunted houses." Schuyler's European friends would prefer roasting Bryant's waterfowl to apostrophizing it, he assures us, perhaps after slaughtering it with "that terrible swift sword so savagely celebrated in the bloodthirsty 'hymn' of one Julia Ward Howe." Clearly, Schuyler's monument to the American centenary is not a work of unalloyed love.

Inasmuch as it was published in 1976, *1876* must also be considered Vidal's monument to the American bicentenary. Vidal aligns the two periods carefully. His Samuel J. Tilden is not unlike George McGovern in many respects, his Rutherford B. Hayes is not unlike Gerald Ford, and his Mark Twain is not unlike the contemporary writer Tom Wolfe.[6] The bicentennial anniversary was haunted by memories of Vietnam, the Kennedy assassination, the Watergate break-ins, and the corrupt Nixon administration; and Vidal's centennial anniversary has its memories of the Civil War, Lincoln's assassination, the Babcock break-in, and the Grant administration.

The violence and mendacity that Schuyler finds prevalent in America in 1876 are perennial flowers in the American garden, but Schuyler and his author do not so much object to the growth of these dubious flowers as object that they grow so messily. Schuyler is never more a cultivated European than when he remarks that flowers belong in vases rather than loose and untidy on the ground, and he is no less the cultivated European in objecting to the untidy measures of American villainy. "I delight in all Bonapartes," he says, "particularly in the first one, whose crimes were on such a large scale that they have ceased to be the stuff of moralizing and are simply history." President Grant would qualify as a Bonaparte in Schuyler's view if Grant's Puritan sense of morality had not made for "confusion."

In a sense, Vidal is inverting Henry James's novelistic formula and looking at corrupt America through the eyes of still-more-corrupt Europe rather than looking at corrupt Europe through the eyes of innocent America. In the same sense, the Princess d'Agrigente is an inverted Jamesian heroine, and the stylistic contrast is significant between her quietly macabre dispatch of Sanford's first wife (assuming the fact) and the too obvious machinations of American politicos. Europe may be capable of darker deeds than America, but that is because in Europe evil is a fact of civilized life, whereas in America immorality is a rude and grubby theater.

A sustained theatrical conceit runs through Vidal's American trilogy. Senator Day sees life at crucial moments as a Shakespearean play in *Washington, D.C.*, and he retires from politics "because he felt that the time had come for him to cease to be an actor." Schuyler had once thought of becoming an actor too, but the newspaper he works for in *Burr* is a "stage more important than that of the Bowery Theatre," and he cannot hope to match the performances of Clay, Jefferson, and others on the Senate floor. Appropriately, the Bowery Theatre changes its name to the "American Theatre" in the course of *Burr,* and Burr's home at Richmond Hill is converted into a theater after he debuts as a villain in the Hamilton farce.

1876 is replete with such allusions. Washington is a "peculiar theatre," and its politicians gesture "like Edwin Forrest as Othello confronting Iago," leave the congressional chamber "like Hamlet in the last act," and conduct themselves "like the very worst sort of actors trying to look like Roman senators." Shakespearean tragedy is the republic's mime, then, although Schuyler says that American politics is really "an ongoing comedy" liable at any moment to become "wildest farce," and he sees himself as playing "the part of foolish elder sage, of Falstaff," at another time, Polonius.

This theatrical conceit is broadly applicable to the world of *1876.* The New York cityscape is something of a scrim, with whorehouses lurking behind cigar store Indians, and the mansion of a wealthy abortionist sitting demurely next to St. Patrick's

Cathedral. With similar effect, ragged, emaciated children paw through trash cans on the fashionable Ladies' Mile of Broadway, and Civil War veterans beg coins beside the red carpet thrown down profligately in the snow for Mrs. William Astor's guests. The homes of New York society are scrims, too, dowdy brownstone without, gilt and tapestry to rival Versailles within. People in New York society are scrims incarnate: Ward McAllister claims an impossible French ancestry; Governor Tilden secretly collects erotic literature; William Sanford is at one moment a "plain-spoken man of the people, all hideously self-made" and at another the "thoughtful Darwinist and social historian"; Mrs. Paran Stevens (of "Chateau Stevens") has even had her portrait painted in the likeness of Madame Sans-Gêne. In fashionable Newport, society women style their mansions "cottages," and though they are "Watteau ladies," they pretend to be "Breughel women" as they convey their chefs' contributions to rustic picnics. In a world of scrims, imposture must even be assumed. Senator Roscoe Conkling's look of sincerity was "so perfectly convincing," Schuyler says, "that I knew myself to be in the presence of a truly deceitful man."

Given the elaborate deceits of the age, Schuyler faces a problem in trying to write its history. Vidal sees a solution, however, in Schuyler's readiness to see the scrims and to suppose the worst. Since the truth is never plainly shown, fantasy and conjecture are necessary approaches to the truth, and since the truth would not have been suppressed were it not scandalous, the more invidious one supposes the truth, the more accurate one is apt to be.[7]

Vidal's spokesman for the first half of this dubious proposition is Baron Jacobi, a diplomatic minister from Bulgaria who enters the world of *1876* via

Henry Adams's novel *Democracy*. The Baron argues that history is something we *cannot* know. What we think to be history is fiction, he maintains, because the historian's raw materials—letters, diaries, and newspaper reports—are "more apt than not to lie." In the Baron's view, one learns about the past from Shakespeare, whose historical characters are "right" whatever Shakespeare's penchant for getting their history wrong. The Baron does not go further (although he might) and observe that Shakespeare's most villainous characters are his most authentic; rather, it is Vidal, through his own dedicated enterprise, through the fact of his writing *1876* and the other novels in the trilogy, who asserts that the most malicious speculations about history are worthwhile and probably accurate. And just as Shakespeare's characters are true because they are "right," so Vidal's characters can claim historical accuracy to the degree that they are credible human beings rather than the plaster idols that have come down to us in the official histories.[8]

If American history is theater, as the conceit suggests, what other truth can there be than the truth of the successful illusion, whether Shakespeare's or Vidal's? What is the "truth" of the history books if public figures are professional illusionists? Such questions are disingenuously posed, of course, but they constitute the essential spirit of the novels in the American trilogy, and they are a marvelous justification of Vidal's naughtiness vis-à-vis American history.

It is ironical in the face of all this that Charles Schuyler is not adequately real as a character. To an extent, he suffers from an inevitable comparison with Burr. Having established Schuyler as a foil to Burr in the earlier novel, Vidal does not develop him in *1876* to the extent that he can command center stage once Burr is dead. Schuyler's judgments on America tend to be incidental and miscellaneous compared to Burr's radical debunking, and his speculations about what is going on behind the scenes are effete compared with Burr's overarching speculations.

Schuyler is, in fact, very much an American innocent behind his European scrim. He is innocent enough to hope Emma innocent, and he is innocent enough to express the belief that "somewhere in this corrupt and canting American society there still exists in certain men a sense of what the good society must be." This innocence does Schuyler enormous damage as a character, for it means that the novel's profound cynicism washes over his head like a great wave, although the novel's cynicism—that is to say, Vidal's cynicism—is technically Schuyler's own. This is not just Vidalian irony. Because the novel is so loosely structured and scatters its anathemas so randomly, it very much needs a narrator who can rise to its cynicism and pull its scattered energies together. The effect of Schuyler's innocence, however, is to compromise his ability to do these things, and the net effect is to compromise his reality as a character. He is so much less than the novel needs him to be that he seems not enough at all according to the ruthless economics of art, not "real" and not true.

In the context of Vidal's three-volume sequence, however, Schuyler's inadequacy as a narrator is well calculated. The three novels move in their chronological order from vigorous old Burr through weary Charles Schuyler down to indolent Peter Sanford at the end of the family line. A decline in the sexual performance, general health, and intellectual vitality of the three protagonists is as carefully gradated as the decline in their physical stamina and age and as carefully gradated, too, as the rapacity of the American politico. A decline in the republic's genes is clearly the point, and it is wholly appropriate in this regard that Schuyler's role as the narrator of *1876* is less dominant than his father's role in *Burr* yet more dominant than Peter's role in *Washington, D.C.* This pattern of the trilogy simply takes precedence over the formal demands of *1876*.

But *1876* is a sophisticated jaunt through the centennial year nonetheless. Who but Vidal would bring Schuyler back to America after thirty-eight years and have him say, "The fact that I can no longer tell a prostitute from a true lady is the first sign that I have been away for a very long time. As a boy, I always knew"? Who except Vidal (and Borges) would say, "Well, the writer is not unlike the explorer. We, too, are searching for lost cities, rare tigers, the sentence never before written"? Indeed, who but Vidal consistently writes such marvelous sentences? *1876* may be a misfired salute to the American (bi)centenary, but even misfires can delight those who have a taste for accomplished prose.

6
The Breckinridge Novels

Myra Breckinridge and its sequel, *Myron,* are Vidal's most entertaining works of fiction. Censured for their sexual preoccupations, they have seldom been taken seriously, and a film version of *Myra Breckinridge* in ludicrously bad taste has not enhanced their reputation. The novels are also about Hollywood and are tainted, therefore, by that curious prejudice that assumes that every novel about Hollywood is no better than a gossip column. Nonetheless, *Myra Breckinridge* and *Myron* are very fine novels, full of high style and good humor, and they are probably the most important novels about Hollywood since Nathanael West's *The Day of the Locust* (1939). I rank them as Vidal's best work.

Myra Breckinridge (1968) takes the form of a journal that the eponymous Myra begins when she goes to Hollywood to lay claim to the landholdings of Buck Loner, a retired horse opera star. She claims that she is the widow of Buck's nephew, Myron Breckinridge, but she is really Myron himself via a sex-change operation. Buck delays settling Myra's claim and tells the story of their legal wrangle on recording discs, simulated transcriptions of which intersperse Myra's journal. As a temporary appeasement, however, Buck appoints Myra an instructor in his Academy of Drama and Modeling, and Myra is delighted to gain this foothold in Hollywood, for she is a motion picture aficionado, encyclopedic in her knowledge of cinematic history, firm in her opinion that film is the only art, and militant in her esteem for Hollywood's Golden Age. *"In the decade between 1935 and 1945, no irrelevant film was made in the United States,"* she boldly declaims, and "celluloid, *blessed* celluloid" is the sort of phrase she often affects.

Myra's delight with Hollywood soon takes second place, however, to her feminist determination to realign the sexes, a determination apparently rooted in her former life as Myron. "No man will ever possess Myra Breckinridge," she insists, "though she will possess men, in her own good time and in ways convenient to her tyrannous lust." A student named Rusty Godowsky tests this determination when he flaunts his manhood in one of Myra's classes, and so Myra sets out to subjugate him, embarking on a series of sexual humiliations which build slowly to a climactic rape scene, with Rusty strapped to a table and Myra triumphantly astride him with a dildo.

Oh, it was a holy moment! I was one with the Bacchae, with all the priestesses of the dark bloody cults, with the great goddess herself for whom Attis unmanned himself. I was the eternal feminine made flesh, the source of life and its destroyer, dealing with man as incidental toy, whose blood as well as semen is needed to make me whole!

As part of the humiliation of Rusty, Myra also attempts to seduce his girl friend, Mary-Ann Pringle, but Mary-Ann has no taste for a lesbian relationship, and Myra is unsuccessful until she is the victim of a hit-and-run accident that reverses her sex change and causes Myron to revive physiologically. Inexplicably, Myron *redivivus* is heterosexual and something of a prig. Mary-Ann prefers him to Myra, however, and so she and Myron eventually settle down in wedded bliss to raise dogs in the San Fernando Valley. "It is a proven fact," Myron illogically concludes, "that happiness, like the proverbial bluebird, is to be found in your own backyard if you just know where to look."

Myra Breckinridge cannot properly be appreciated unless it is understood as "camp," and the taste for camp literature is a special one, by no means common. As Susan Sontag points out in her classic notes on the subject, the sensibility attuned to camp delights in artifice as such.[1] It relishes especially artifice that is exaggerated and intensely mannered, such as the Art Nouveau lamp that mimics a grapevine or a tree. Camp differs from comedy and satire in that the response it invites to such artifice is appreciative, not critical. Ultimately, the camp sensibility views the serious artifice frivolously and the frivolous artifice solemnly, not in a spirit of perversity but because the odd angle of approach freshens the viewpoint and redeems artifice otherwise unappreciable.

Myra's notion of herself as "disturbingly beautiful" is camp in this sense, for it is a triumph of the heightened manner, perfectly sustained and ludicrously founded. At the beginning of the novel she promises to give the reader

an exact, literal sense of what it is like, from moment to moment, to be me, what it is like to possess superbly shaped breasts reminiscent of those sported by Jean Harlow in *Hell's Angels* and seen at their best four minutes after the start of the second reel. What it is like to possess perfect thighs. . . .

Myra's ravishment by her own beauty extends

even to her odor ("like that of new bread") and to her
feet ("lovely feet with a high instep and naturally
rosy heels, fit for any fetishist"). The femmes fatales
of Hollywood's Golden Age do not shake her confidence, for she believes she can match them point for
point. She laughs as delightfully as Carole Lombard,
she assures us; she whispers as excitingly as Phyllis
Thaxter; and she smiles as winningly as Ann Sothern.
She can project at will the compassion of Kay Francis, she says, or the warmth of June Allyson, or the
sweetness of Irene Dunne. Effectively, it is her conceit that she is the archetypal femme fatale, and she
carries off the conceit without apology for the silicone and the hormones that have made it possible.

Although this conceit is the heart of the novel's
camp appeal, Myra also says such things as "no man
alive can outdo *me* in the huskiness department,"
and such remarks introduce an androgynous note
that cuts across the grain of her femme fatale performance. Indeed, Myra plays both drill sergeant and
sex kitten in the novel. If she wears black mesh un-
dergarments and refuses to wear glasses, she also
prides herself on her "one-two punch" and her ability to force strong men to their knees. "I do share the
normal human response to whatever is attractive
physically in either sex," she asserts, but even this
claim to bisexuality is camp, inasmuch as she and
Myron share a single androgynous body.

Ultimately, we must even wonder which of
Myra's two selves sodomizes Rusty. It is Myra, in an
act of brutal feminist heterosexuality? Or is it Myron,
covertly asserting his homosexuality under the cover
of Myra's heterosexuality? And who tries to seduce
Mary-Ann? Is it the Myra who claims to be bisexual,
or is it a Myra who has inherited Myron's homosexuality and refocused it as lesbianism? Is it perhaps
Myron *redivivus*, flaunting his heterosexuality

prematurely? Such questions are not disingenuous, for the androgyn, the sex goddess, and the closet queen struggle for dominance in Myra's psyche. They struggle even in Myra's lingering fondness for Myron. "How I miss him!" she says several times, only to remark, "Yet, all in all, he is better dead," showing that she is wary of allowing him his share in her psyche. Myra's tendency to speak of herself in the third person suggests still another possibility, that Myron has difficulty sustaining an imposture as Myra. The whole tedious conundrum is extravagantly camp —an apotheosis of the epicene.

Myra's outsize sensibility owes a great deal to her hero, the real-life film critic Parker Tyler. Specifically, her notion that she is an archetypal femme fatale takes its cue from Tyler's *Magic and Myth of the Movies* (1947), a book which is devoted to Hollywood mythopoesis and which Myra quotes several times.[2] In fact, Myra's esteem for such minor Hollywood actresses as Betty Hutton is borrowed intact from Tyler, although Myra is insensitive to Tyler's camping and mistakes his surrealistic flights of fancy for authentic valuations. Myra's prose style is also indebted to Tyler, especially her wacky generalizations and exact film citations ("four minutes after the start of the second reel"), which mimic the interplay in Tyler's writings between towering theory and minute analysis. In short, Tyler's camp view of the Hollywood film is the model for Myra's camp view of herself. Both are awesomely holistic; both are absurdly fragile.

Myra also owes a stylistic debt to Alain Robbe-Grillet, the dean of the French New Novelists, for she tries conscientiously to imitate Robbe-Grillet's prose in her journal by restricting herself to physical description and by avoiding subjective analysis as much as she is able. Such a puristic style is hopelessly un-

suited to Myra's hyperbolic and obsessive self-con-
sciousness, however, and so her intermittent attempts at this style fail in the same way that the Art
Nouveau lamp fails when it tries to imitate a grapevine.

I have covered eighteen pages already; that leaves two
hundred eighty-two to be filled, if one counts the present
page of which I have used twelve of thirty-two lines—
thirteen with these last words, now fourteen. The hand is
small, with delicate tapering fingers and a slight golden
down at the back near the wrist. The nails are exquisitely
cared for (lacquered silver) except for the right index
fingernail, which is cracked diagonally from the left side of
the tip to the part where the flesh begins, the result of
trying to pry loose an ice cube from one of those new
plastic ice trays which so freeze that unless you half melt
them under the hot-water tap you can never get the ice
out.

The passage is an incidental parody of Robbe-
Grillet's novel *Jealousy* (1958), but in its shift to rhap-
sodic self-appreciation and in its climactic displea-
sure with a post-1945 ice tray, it is quintessential
Myra Breckinridge as much as it is mock Robbe-Grillet, and it is to that extent the sheerest camp.
What is often adjudged pornographic in the
novel is also camp, particularly the sodomizing of
Rusty. Obviously, Vidal deploys all the clichés of pornographic literature in that central scene: the slow
disrobing; the gourmet response to buttocks, nipples,
and pubic hair; the diddling of the testes en route to
the sphincter. For the fetishist, Vidal even serves up
jockey shorts and bondage. Nonetheless, the rape is
essentially camp, for the titillation is so slick and
mannered that the clichés assert themselves precisely as clichés, losing their force as stimuli and gaining
appreciability as artifice. Myra is simply being Myra,
as flamboyantly a dominatrix as she is a femme fatale,

as stylishly carnal as she is feminist; everything in the
rape scene springs from her irrepressible, virtually
uncontrolled sensibility. Thus, the pornographic
clichés seem the innocent overflow of her high spirits, however paradoxically. Indeed, Myra herself is as
endearing in the rape scene as when she awakens in
the hospital toward the end of the novel and cries out
imperiously, "Where are my breasts? *Where are my
breasts?*" Her sense of high style justifies everything,
at least to the camp sensibility.

Because of these camp pleasures of *Myra Breckinridge*, I tend to forgive the novel its glaring faults:
the laziness of its boomerang ending, Rusty's unreal-
istic submission in the rape scene, Buck Loner's tedious interruptions of the text. Probably because the
camp aesthetic transcends the good-bad categories
of ordinary literary judgment, these flaws in the architecture of the novel do not seem important. Myra
survives them as she survives the canons of orthodox
morality and good taste, breastless to be sure, but
ebullient, *démesuré*, and gloriously herself.

Myron (1974) picks up the story of Myron Breckinridge in 1973, five years after we leave him in *Myra
Breckinridge*, but the novel begins with Myron's
shocked discovery that he has been transplanted to
1948. While fiddling with the volume knob on his
television set, he suddenly experienced "this awful
pushing and sucking sensation" and found himself
inside the TV, watching the original filming of *Siren
of Babylon*, a motion picture he had been watching
in 1973 in his rumpus room.[3] It is of course Myra, his
transsexual succubus, who has arranged this marvel.
"There is nothing," she says, "I don't know about
how to break into the movies."

As the novel proceeds, Myra and Myron alternately repossess the fractured Breckinridge psyche

and come to the fore as narrator. Myron wants only to return to his wife, his dogs, and his Chinese catering business, but Myra feels a mission to save Hollywood from the imminent threat of television. Thus she tampers with *Siren of Babylon*, introducing subliminal touches of nudity to give the film an appeal at the box office that it never had, and she even tries to insinuate herself into the higher councils of MGM through her foreknowledge of gross receipts. As a Malthusian, she also feels a mission to reduce the 1973 population, and so she attempts to castrate a young actor named Steve Dude. That attempt is unsuccessful because Myron interrupts her, but Myra later succeeds in vasectomizing an unsuspecting extra in *Siren of Babylon*. She calculates that if she could vasectomize all 300 male extras in *Siren of Babylon*, she would spare the world 690 new citizens by 1973.

There are approximately eighty persons on the set of *Siren of Babylon* who have emigrated unwittingly from the future by falling into their televisions. Among them are a hairdresser from White Plains who calls himself Maude and becomes Myra's special ally, supplying her with makeup and wardrobe, and a crazed homosexual named Whittaker Kaiser (a caricature of Norman Mailer) who becomes Myron's special friend. A mysterious Mr. Williams (Henry James) presides over the emigrés by virtue of being the first of them to arrive on the MGM back lot, and Myra becomes his implacable foe when she realizes that he champions books and is feeding bad advice to MGM as part of a campaign to destroy the film industry. She decides that *Siren of Babylon* must be a smash hit if Williams is to be defeated, and so she attempts to remove Maria Montez's breastplate during a commercial freeze so that the star will appear topless in the completed film. Myra miscalculates her

timing, however, and accidentally *becomes* Maria
Montez when the filming resumes, while Montez
takes up residence in ten-year-old Myron, somewhat
to the consternation of his mother.

But all this is undone when "Maria Montez"
makes a public appearance at the grand opening of
a local department store, and young Myron and his
mother are among the opening-day crowd. The real
Maria Montez seizes the opportunity to become herself again, and, in the mysterious economy of such
things, Myron is catapulted back to his rumpus room
just in time to see the last frames of *Siren of Babylon*
unroll. The novel concludes, then, with Myron holding sway over Myra once again. We are assured in a
final slip of Myron's pen, however, that *"!sevil aryM."*

Sequels have a sorry reputation, and so it is not
surprising that *Myron* tends automatically to be
thought inferior to *Myra Breckinridge,* an effort, as it
were, to prolong unnaturally Myra's unnatural life.
In a few respects, perhaps, *Myron* is a disappoint-
ment after the earlier novel. In a mock show of inoffensiveness, Vidal systematically replaces genital
vulgarisms with the names of the Supreme Court
justices who ruled that obscenity is determined by
local standards, and such sophomoric wit is markedly
inferior to anything in *Myra Breckinridge.* The wit is
sophomoric, too, when Richard Nixon shows up on
MGM's back lot, wanting to know if 1948 has an
extradition treaty with the future, for such jokes
about Nixon were too easy in the Watergate context
and much too predictable a flourish in Vidal's writings of the period. The minor characters in *Myron*
also suffer somewhat in a comparison of the two novels, for they are less organically essential to the plot
than the minor characters in *Myra Breckinridge* and
not nearly so successful as sexual archetypes.

Nonetheless, *Myron* is a more richly imagined

work.[4] Consider, for instance, the complex time-and-space fantasy which Vidal uses to suggest Myron's experience of living inside *Siren of Babylon*. When Myron positions himself on the camera side of the filming action, he experiences the eight-week making of the film in 1948, complete with technicians bustling about and stars sweating under heavy make-up. Time is relatively slow in this dimension, for there are frequent longueurs while the 1973 screening freezes the 1948 time frame for a commercial. (It is during one such commercial that Myra vasecto-mizes a frozen extra.) But when Myron positions himself at the edge of the filming activity, he experiences the film as it unreels in 1973 on television, and the effects of this positioning in time and space are very different. Myron is violently knocked about during the rush of the credits; he experiences a terrible sense of bifurcation during a "DISSOLVE TO"; and he develops the heebie-jeebies when the MGM lion looms thirty times life size. The further Myron backs up behind the camera, however, the more slowly the film unreels, and if he backs up halfway across MGM's back lot, he is still in 1945 but relatively disas-sociated from the movie. Yet *Siren of Babylon* is always visible in the background, as is appropriate, unwinding in a slow, eight-week screening that cor-responds to the eight weeks the film was in produc-tion.

This elaborate time-and-space fantasy is won-drously devised, just logical enough in its arrange-ments to tease one's conceptions of time and space and just mad enough to illumine the erratic but pris-tine logic of Myra's obsessions. What better forum, after all, for Myra to work out her adoration of Holly-wood's tackiest films than the Golden Age itself? What more fitting obsession for a Malthusian trans-sexual than healthy testes, circa 1948? And what bet-

ter measure of Myra's prodigious will to save MGM
from going broke than her prodigious transcendence
of time and space?

Vidal also invents innumerable ploys to allow
Myra her camp disquisitions on Hollywood. When
she inadvertently turns into Maria Montez, Myra
finds herself married to the French actor Jean-Pierre
Aumont, and she remarks of the mésalliance: "Not
only does he keep talking French to me but the only
people we ever see in this town are *not* Lana, Judy,
Bette and Dolores Moran, who are at their zenith,
but all the goddamned French actors like Charles
Boyer. . . ." Her foreknowledge allows her to give
Judy Garland some pointed advice about drugs and
alcohol and to suggest that Joanne Woodward
cribbed her Oscar-winning performance in *Three
Faces of Eve* from Myra's stellar performance as herself. Greta Garbo, Myra says airily, "was *not* truly
Hollywood as a comparison with, say, her contemporary Lana Turner would quickly demonstrate and to
Miss G's disadvantage." The most charming moment
in the novel occurs when Myra spots William Eythe
and Lon McCallister in the street. "I confess that
when I recognized them, I screamed," she blushing-
ly admits. "But then I am afraid that I started to *run*
after their car. Yes, I lost my head!" Somewhere in
the tangles of the Breckinridge psyche, apparently,
Myra is still a bobby-soxer clutching her autograph
album.

The sexual shenanigans in *Myron* are certainly
inventive, considering Myra's efforts to create a race
of fun-loving Amazons, her humiliation of a would-be
rapist, and her statistical surveys of male genitalia.
Not above a little commercial speculation, she even
considers selling the formula for silicone some years
before it is developed, certain that there are thou-
sands of transsexuals who need proper breasts. The

novel has nothing so memorable as the rape of Rusty Godowsky, but it has a rape scene that recalls it, even to the extent that the victim, Steve Dude, is referred to as "Red." As we have seen, however, Vidal affects a mock restraint in *Myron*, and so he gives us a gamy description of foreplay before the rape but pulls a curtain over the rape itself. Myron's preemption of the Breckinridge psyche just as Myra prepares to castrate Dude is another instance of this tongue-in-cheek morality; Vidal *apparently* has conceded that enough is enough. Vidal concedes no such thing, of course, and Myron is punished for his interference by having to confront Dude, who is still handcuffed to the bed and still full of obliging "Yes, ma'am's." In a sense, Myron's embarrassed takeover midway between the rape and the castration is Vidal's revenge on those who objected to the rape scene in *Myra Breckinridge*, for Myron is their machismo-minded surrogate, sexually suspect in his dishabille and entirely out of his depth.

The especial advantage of Myron's sexuality being pitted so nakedly against Myra's is that their enmity inspires a gaudy fireworks of invective, quite superior to the exchanges between Buck Loner and Myra in *Myra Breckinridge*. Obscenities and recriminations shoot freely back and forth as the antagonists settle down to a stalemated war, and tweezered eyebrows, padded brassieres, and raw oysters become delightful beachheads in their battle for sexual supremacy. Myron's hairiness even becomes as much of a battle cry as Myra's breasts. Myron threatens Myra that he will take male hormones and turn the Breckinridge body as hairy as a tarantula, a prospect little to Myra's taste, and she threatens him that she will dance the tarantella in a Maidenform bra, more or less on his grave. Almost anything can set the fireworks off. Although "Myra" is an anagram of

"Mary," the generic name queens use in addressing one another, Maude lights an unexpected fuse when he says to Myra, "I've known many a drag queen in my day, sweetie, but you're the tops."

I could not let that low blow go unparried. "Maude," I said, achieving that very special vocal quality which has been known to make the marrow of the cockiest stud turn to water. "I am not a drag queen. Repeat: I am not that most ridiculous of creatures. I am Myra Breckinridge. Admittedly damaged, mutilated but, Maude, *unbowed!* The anomaly, the imposter, the travesty is *Myron* Breckinridge.

But of course Myron is just as insulted to be thought a drag queen. He even begins to wear a cowboy outfit and to affect the walk of an arthritic bear to show people that he is "deeply and sincerely butch." Because the composite Breckinridges are in one sense very much a drag queen, this is all charmingly loony, a pyrotechnical display of make-believe sexuality.

The stylistics of the novel are no less gaudy. Myron's prose is hopelessly lumpish and demotic. He is a "straight-shooter," he assures us with a straight face, and he is prone to bursts of soapbox patriotism that make the reader squirm. "The American dream," he says, "has been won for most of us who work hard and support our country and various community churches and organizations throughout this great land of ours in spite of the heavy burden of the people on welfare that we are forced to carry on our shoulders as a result of the crushing tax burden we have inherited from earlier, socialist-minded administrations." The sheer ungainliness of such prose has a perverse charm, and Myron's prose is at its ungainly best on those occasions when Myra fades into his sensibility without entirely preempting him. A boy named Chicken Van Upp, the son of Myron's concierge, inspires one such occasion, and Myron fondly imagines

a real sort of palship between Chicken Van Upp and yours truly, consisting of us two fishing for trout in one of your nearby streams, skinny-dipping together in the old swimming hole the way it used to be when a man and a boy and a dog, too, sometimes, could have a real relationship without your real boy like Chicken ending up stuffed from behind like an olive with a pimento like Steve Dude.

This is devilishly inept, with its crass "palship" and voguish "relationship," its conjunction of "Upp" and "yours," its suggestive allusions to skinny-dipping and holes, and its hint of bestiality. The final simile is simply appalling—only the unfortunate cadences of the passage are *more* appalling—and the name "Chicken" is neatly appropriate, inasmuch as it is both homosexual slang for a young male and conventional slang for one fearful of joining in.

Myra's prose, on the other hand, is decadently overripe, full of syntactic crescendos and baroque cadences, its saving grace a strain of funkiness that cuts through the overripeness like a knife. Whittaker Kaiser has the temerity to give her the eye, Myra says, and she typically adds, "if that tiny red oyster so like to an infected buttonhole could be said to have any *interpretable* expression." On the subject of the novel, Myra is giddily eloquent.

I confess that in my day I have studied the enemy, contemplated the strategies of fiction if only in order to find new ways to destroy the art form whose only distinction is that it prepared the way for the movies, much as John the B. prepared the way for big J. C. And of course I will never deny the importance of *any* novel which has been used to inspire a work of celluloid. We are all permanently indebted to James Hilton, Daphne du Maurier and W. Somerset Maugham, whose names head the golden list. Yet at their best their works are no more than so much grit beneath the studio's shell: mere occasions for masterpieces, for cinema pearls.

Indeed, there are as many styles in *Myron* as their are sexualities, and all of them are nicely overcooked. Mr. Williams says, "For me, even as we speak, the golden bowel has begun ever so slightly to most beautifully crack," and we hear the voice of Henry James, slightly vulgarized. Myra says, "My fellow Americans. . . . If I succeed in this great enterprise, I vow to you that the moral rot at the center of the United States will be nipped in the bud," and we hear the unmistakable accents of Richard Nixon. Whittaker Kaiser says, "Look, every man wants to make it with another man but the *real* man is the one who fights this hideous weak fag self and takes one woman after another without the use of any contraceptives or pill or diaphragm or rubber, just the all-conquering sperm because contraception of any kind is as bad as masturbation. . . ." In this we hear the avalanche of Norman Mailer's prose. It is an enormously rich diet—a comedic feast of styles and sexualities, invention and invective—a diet somewhat richer than *Myra Breckinridge* offers, although Myra herself is still the incomparable *pièce de résistance*.

Behind the fun of the Breckinridge novels lurks a certain anger, perhaps, and a certain impatience with the connections between power and sex. There are also semiserious links in the novels between American politics and Hollywood-style fantasy, as when Myra links the dread Peckinpah's corruption of film to the Nixon Presidency. But it would be a mistake to overemphasize such elements and treat the novels as serious political tracts, pandering to inconsequential interests only to gain our attention. The charm of the novels is precisely their balletic flights of inconsequence. They are preposterous, droll, gaudily offensive—altogether triumphant and altogether wonderful.

7
The Essays

Vidal has generally earned high marks as an essayist —so high, in fact, that it is increasingly fashionable to regard him as a first-rate essayist and a second-rate novelist.[1] He is certainly a prolific essayist, having published over a hundred pieces in magazines and journals of opinion, and it is generally agreed that he is one of the major essayists writing in English today. Collections of his essays have appeared with regularity. *Rocking the Boat* appeared in 1962, *Sex, Death and Money* in 1968, *Reflections Upon a Sinking Ship* in 1969, *Homage to Daniel Shays: Collected Essays 1952–1972* in 1972, and *Matters of Fact and of Fiction (Essays 1973–1976)* in 1977.

As one would anticipate, many of Vidal's essays reflect the interests of his novels. Essays on the Caesars, on the Adams family, and on President and Mrs. Ulysses S. Grant echo the subjects of *Julian, Burr,* and *1876,* and such essays as "Pornography," "The Death of Mishima," and "Sex and the Law" reflect the sexual hypotheses of *The City and the Pillar* and *Myra Breckinridge.* A number of essays on literary subjects can be read as apologias for Vidal's own fiction, such as "Novelists and Critics of the 1940's" and "American Plastic: The Matter of Fiction." Smaller themes cut insistently through these larger interests. We read frequently of Vidal's contempt for "book-chat" writers, for academicians, and for *The New York Times*. We read of his concerns with overpopulation and big business. We read time and again about his maternal grandfather, the late Senator Gore of Oklahoma.

But the most frequent subject of Vidal's essays is what he calls "the American imperium"—a confederation of power brokers and moneyed corporations that covertly rules America and attempts with too much success to rule the world as well. He finds evidence of the imperium not only in the Oval Office and the Chase Manhattan Bank but in the dynastic pretensions of the Kennedy family, the octopus embrace of International Telephone and Telegraph, and the financial ploys of Robert Moses.

Vidal is in fact a vocal critic of the American establishment. He unabashedly refers to Lyndon Johnson as "the master criminal," as "the emperor of the West, the scourge of Asia and shield to ungrateful Europe." Richard Nixon is more simply "First Criminal"; his wife Patricia, "First Moll." "I use the word *Bank*," he says boldly, "as a kind of shorthand not just for the Chase Manhattan but also for the actual ownership of the United States," and he insists that there is only one political party in the country, terming it variously the Property Party and the Banksparty. The nation is in its death throes, Vidal argues, and when the imperium is his specific theme, he envisions economic apocalypse.

I have a feeling that like the joyous [Bernie] Cornfeld's paper pyramid, ITT, too, will pass, taking the currency of the Western world with it in a replay of 1929. So, puritans, take heart. We may be at the end of that paper money which has been for our rulers a puzzling and currently alarming fiat for their much loved barbarous metal; and for the poor, as someone once said, their blood. Absolute purity will then require us to return to the delights and challenges of barter, and to real things.

But Vidal is not really a profound thinker about politics, and most of his essays simply serve up liberal thought of the day. The essay "West Point" is a perfectly standard attack, circa 1970s, on the military-industrial complex, whereas "What Robert Moses Did to New York City" is a standard exposé of a public official. Both are fine essays in the muckraking tradition, but they are not original in either their passion or their politics. A 1961 philippic entitled "Police Brutality" is even embarrassing, so conventional is Vidal's rage over high-handed officers of the law. Indeed, although *realpolitik* is Vidal's theme, the assessment of United States *realpolitik* is not his strength. "For both Lincoln and Grant it was *e pluribus unum* no matter what the price in blood or constitutional rights," he declares, wildly simplifying the issues behind the Civil War. Leaving himself open to a charge of *sancta simplicitas*, he tosses off charges that the United States is a "nation of ongoing hustlers," a "garrison state," a "corrupt society," a "nation that worships psychopaths," and an "armed camp." Even his more temperate opinions seem cavalier at times, as when he argues that legalization of narcotics would remove the Mafia and other big-time dispensers from the drug scene.

The judgments in Vidal's literary essays tend also to be of the garden variety, but the essays "French Letters: Theories of the New Novel" and "Calvino's Novels" are distinguished exceptions. "French Letters" is a shrewd and balanced assessment of the *nouvelle roman*, that curious genre born of French logic, and "Calvino's Novels" is a judicious introduction to a body of work virtually unknown in America. Both essays broke new ground when they were published, and both are lucid, dispassionate studies that pass muster as serious literary criticism.

Most of Vidal's essays on literature are less weighty, however. In an engaging romp through the best-selling books of January 7, 1973, he argues disingenuously that nine of the ten books he surveys show the influence of Hollywood films. One wants to borrow a Joan Crawford riposte Vidal puts conveniently to hand and reply, "Whom is fooling whom?" Similarly, the well-known essays "The Hacks of Academe" and "American Plastic" are lightweight pieces that splenetically denounce so-called academic novels. "There is a black cloth on my head as I write," Vidal murmurs in introducing his remarks on John Barth, and Vidal is indeed a hanging judge in the essays, giving less quarter to such serious writers as Barth, Thomas Pynchon, and Donald Barthelme than to the hacks discussed in "The Top Ten Best Sellers."

Vidal's essays, then, cultivate a deliberate comic inflation rather than orthodoxy and exactitude. Their mode is satire. Vidal's review of the psychologist David Reuben's treatise *Everything You Always Wanted to Know about Sex* argues with typical insouciance that Reuben's style "shifts in a very odd way from night-club comedian to reform rabbi, touching en route almost every base except the scientific." Psychiatry itself, Vidal says, is "somewhere between astrology and phrenology on the scale of human gullibility." This is broad, imprecise categorizing to be sure, but the exaggeration is classically satiric, and its glibness establishes perfectly that Reuben's pseudo-scientific sex manual does not merit Vidal's attention as a reviewer. In other essays Vidal maintains that Richard Nixon is an underestimated wit, and this running conceit functions in much the same way as the Reuben satire, suggesting that the dishonored

President's ideas are uninteresting except as howlers, his Presidency beyond comprehension unless as a joke. In a more earnest vein but still a satiric one, Vidal congratulates the critic Susan Sontag on her corresponding *lack* of humor:

[H]er moral seriousness is considerably enhanced by a perfect absence of humor, that most devastating of gifts usually thrust at birth upon the writer in English. Unhindered by a sense of humor, she is able to travel fast in the highest country, unafraid of appearing absurd, and of course invulnerable to irony.

This is first-rate satire, too. The word "perfect" clearly denotes an imperfection; Sontag's lack of fear, insensibility; her "invulnerability to irony," a lethal wound.

Vidal is in fact always ready to turn a mocking phrase. He assures us in a 1976 essay that the young Truman Capote was no less attractive in his person in 1948 than at present. In another essay he states, "I am usually quick, even eager, to respond to the outrageously funny, the villainously slanderous . . . in short, to *The New York Times* itself." Quoting a passage from Herman Wouk, he comments, "This is not at all bad, except as prose." Vidal is especially skilled at relating anecdotes, and at their best his anecdotes blend iconoclastic satire with wry affection. In "Some Memories of the Glorious Bird," he tells the story of Tennessee Williams informing a group of Jesuits that since his conversion to Roman Catholicism he had felt a divine presence constantly within him:

The Jesuits shifted uneasily at this. Like the old trouper he is, the Bird [Williams] then paused abruptly in midflight in order to see just what effect he was having. After a moment of embarrassed silence, one of the Jesuits asked, timidly, "Is this presence a *warm* presence?"
    "There is," said the Bird firmly, "no temperature."

Under the rubric of satire, Vidal also does a mean imitation. "The lugubrious Southern singsong voice never stopped," he says of Carson McCullers: " 'Did ya see muh lovely play? Did ya lahk muh lovely play? Am Ah gonna win the Pew-litzuh prahzz?' "

The most strategic aspect of Vidal's satire is its tone of mock pomposity. It is the very nature of pomposity *not* to mock itself, of course, and because of this inherent ambiguity, Vidal's pseudo-pomposity assimilates both his liberal clichés and his exaggerations and renders both as much a joke as one cares to understand them. What exactly does Vidal intend, for example, when he says of the critic John Simon that "he is only an Illyrian gangster and is blessedly free of side; he simply wants to torture and kill in order to be as good an American as Mr. Charles Manson, say, or Lyndon Johnson"? The use of "only" and "simply" is obviously ironic, as is the notion that Mr. Simon is free of side, but the grouping of the acerbic Simon with a mass murderer and with "the scourge of Asia" constitutes such egregious overkill that the passage can be understood as spoofing Simon's own tendency to critical overkill. On the other hand, if hating Mr. Simon is one's bent, the passage can also be understood as a particularly venemous attack on his motives.[2] Vidal's mock pomposity is a commodious and durable tone, in short, and it allows him an extraordinary freedom of satiric reference.

This mock pomposity is also a performance in itself—almost a vaudeville performance—and one of the great charms of the essays. The charm emerges particularly in Vidal's tendency to puncture his sentences with a demotic word or two, thereby mocking his self-conscious correctness. In reviewing *The Personal Memoirs of Julia Dent Grant,* he says, "As one reads, in the vast spaces between the lines of Julia's narrative, it would seem that Mrs. Lincoln went ab-

solutely bananas. . . . But, fortunately, Julia was masterful—'I quietly placed my hand on hers'—and was
soothing." "Absolutely bananas" is a shrewd touch in
the context of Julia's empty Victorianisms, for it
raises pertinently the question of her memoir's candor. Perhaps more important, however, it is an enlivening auctorial performance, with Vidal announcing
in effect that he is cutting through the First Lady's
balderdash. In a kindred spirit, Vidal refers to an
eighteenth-century notion that the black races suffer
from a sort of inverted leprosy: "Enlightened opti-
mists like Jefferson's friend the learned Dr. Rush
were certain that advanced dermatology would one
day restore to these dark peoples their lost prettiness." Like "absolutely bananas," "prettiness" is marvelously sappy, and once again it is not only a
rhetorical deflation but an accomplished performance; Vidal the purist has descended to the demotic in his despair over Demos's lunacy. Time and again
Vidal puts on such verbal sackcloth to denounce intellectual and moral incompetence. We must never
allow another President the "fun" of destroying
someone else's country, he cautions. The Seventh
Earl of Longford ("who made me love him as he
loves him") has a "super" time fulminating against
pornographers. Spiro Agnew was acceptable to
political bosses in 1968 because he was "firm with
niggers." Furthering the vaudevillian spirit, goosey
nicknames abound: Alexander Solzhenitsyn is "the
noble engineer"; Vladimir Nabokov, "the black swan
of Swiss-American letters"; Robert Moses, "the King
Lear of Jones Beach."

Yet I am not prepared to say, with the fashion,
that Vidal's essays are better than his novels. The two
seem to me very much alike. Just as the novels typically find their strength in the small scene rather
than the large plot, so the essays are more interesting

for their quips, their anecdotes, and their satirical exaggerations than for the spine of essayistic logic that these bend to their will. The essays, like the novels, are a banquet of canapés. They may leave one hungry for logical fair play, as the novels leave one hungry for plot, but the canapés are so tasty withal that more conventional fare seems unflavored. It is perhaps relevant that Vidal was once asked if writing *Myra Breckinridge* was the same experience as writing an essay about William Buckley. His answer? "Sure."[3]

8
The Minor Works

Although Vidal had several early successes, he was almost two decades into his career before he discovered his most successful voices and the literary forms that would best accommodate them. The novels, scripts, and short stories that he produced en route to those discoveries bear the scars of experimentation, but they merit brief attention inasmuch as they are the workshop in which the Vidalian manner was forged.

In a Yellow Wood (1947) was Vidal's second novel, and it is based on his brief stint as an editor in the New York offices of E. P. Dutton and Company. The central character is Robert Holton, a young veteran employed in a Manhattan brokerage firm, and the novel deals with twenty-four hours in Holton's life. His days are dull and unvaried as a rule, but Holton rather likes them that way. His mechanical politeness and his industriousness are the habits of a man obsessed with himself in an unimaginative way, and it is symptomatic of Holton's profound blandness that Vidal enlivens the first half of his day by watching him through the eyes of others, each of whom has his own chapter and *vita*. The watchers include Marjorie Ventusa, the waitress who serves him breakfast and lunch; Caroline Lawson, a secretary in his office; Dick Kuppleton, a clerk who suspects that Holton is after his job; Oliver Murphy, the head of his department; and Lawrence Heywood, an owner of the firm. All these characters are fascinated by Holton, for they mistake his blandness for subtlety. They are as shallow as he, however, and their interest in Holton counts for little.

A slight disturbance enters Holton's day during the early afternoon with the surprise appearance of his old Army friend, Jim Trebling, for Trebling reminds Holton of more adventurous plans they had once made for their lives. And in the early evening Holton meets the exotic Florentine, Carla Bankton, whom he had loved in Italy during the war. Like Trebling, Carla is a shock to Holton's postwar detachment, for she evokes a world where life was vital and love was important. When Holton and Carla have drinks at a homosexual nightclub, Holton is mildly shocked again both by the liberated antics at the nightclub and by one homosexual's declaration that "identities are the only real things we have." Holton makes love to Carla that evening in response to the shocks of the day, but he will not marry her as she wants, and he leaves her in the morning to return to the dull routine of Wall Street, where his nonidentity is secure.

The novel's title derives from a Robert Frost poem "The Road Not Taken," in which Frost's narrator says that he was once faced with two roads diverging "in a yellow wood" and had to choose between them. Holton is in that yellow wood (the brokerage firm is named "Heywood and Golden"), and he must choose between marching in place on Wall Street and ambling more vitally down the path reopened by Trebling and Carla. He chooses Wall Street at the climax of the novel, but his determination to become a broker at that point is no stronger than at the beginning of the novel, and so a sense of déjà vu eclipses his decision. Indeed, his decision is a considerable problem in the narrative. On the one hand Vidal never convinces us that Holton seriously considers the adventurous paths Trebling and Carla open to him, and on the other hand he does not allow us to see Holton as a poseur, merely affecting to face a difficult choice. Admittedly, Holton spends an inordinate amount of time looking in mirrors, but he is not dramatizing himself in the mirrors so much as taking inventory, like the unimaginative clerk he is. At the end of the novel he even fails to find his image in a mirror, and then, we are told, "the reflection of his face appeared in the mirror and he looked at it without interest because it was familiar and because he could see nothing behind it." To the degree that this scene is emblematic of Holton's relationship with himself, the whole crisis in the yellow wood seems concocted, and to that same degree the novel seems hollow at its core.

Vidal himself thinks ill of the novel. *"In a Yellow Wood* is in limbo forever," he remarked in 1974. "I can't rewrite it because it's so bad that I can't reread it."[1] The novel can certainly be faulted not only for its hollow core but also for the slickness of its characterizations and the triteness of its symbolism. It is a basically competent narrative, however. If the novel's naturalistic style is inferior Hemingway, the style is suited to Holton's spiritual emptiness, and if the novel's plot is rigidly schematic, one wishes that some of Vidal's better novels were as tightly controlled. Indeed, there are touches in the novel that are artful, as when the narrator refers to Holton by his forename in the scenes with Carla, the change from the customary surname suggesting that Holton is on the verge of selfhood. The verbal wit of Vidal's

mature style glimmers fitfully through the straitjack-
eted prose. Apropos of Caroline's scorn for New
York, we are told that her laugh leveled the buildings
and cracked Grant's Tomb, and when the office
receptionist says, "I wouldn't worry about what nob
. . . anybody thought," Holton responds in a rare
moment of wit, "That's what I used to say."

   The Season of Comfort (1949) centers on a young
man named Bill Giraud and traces the first eighteen
years of his life. They are disturbing years, for incest
and generational conflicts smolder in Giraud's family
and tend to burn through the surface of its Southern
gentility. Indeed, the novel traces the tangle of emotional relationships in the family as much as it traces
Bill's story. A great deal of attention is given to Senator Hawkins, Bill's grandfather, and to the loyalty he
inspires as the family patriarch. Clara Hawkins, the
senator's wife, commands an even larger share of
attention. A slightly embittered wallflower for most
of her married life, she is appointed to fill her husband's unexpired term of office after his death, and
she comes suddenly and gloriously into her own.
   Their daughter Charlotte is the novel's villain.
She loves her father for his political success, but she
has only contempt for her mother, and Clara Hawkins responds in kind, unable to abide Charlotte's
willfulness, egotism, and rivalry for Senator Hawkins's love. The two women are also rivals over the
memory of a dead family son. To Clara her dead son
was the loving male that the senator is not and the
loving child that Charlotte is not; to Charlotte, who
loved her dead brother incestuously, he was the ideal
man in every way. Given such hero worship of her
brother, Charlotte is naturally a shrewish wife. She
continually nags Stephen Giraud, her first husband,
about his lack of vitality, and she finally divorces him

to marry wealthy Roger Gilray; she then nags Gilray
about his "lack of consideration" and divorces him in
turn. Bill Giraud is the child of Charlotte and Stephen Giraud, and he absorbs the brunt of Charlotte's
shrewishness when no one else is at hand. His task in
the novel is to be free of her.

The novel is organized in terms of seven discontinuous days, each corresponding to a chapter. Some
of the days are conventionally important, like the
days of Bill's birth, christening, and graduation from
preparatory school. Other days have a significance
more personal to Bill. Almost every chapter is per-
meated with flashbacks, however, and through their
agency Bill's story is sketched more fully than the
distantly spaced days might suggest. We learn of
Bill's initiation into schoolboy sex and his decision to
be the painter his father aspired to be; we learn of his
increasing respect for his father, despite Charlotte's
attacks on his character; we learn of Bill's growing
commitment to a girl decidedly unlike his mother.
The novel's theme is voiced in its final line: "Spring,
like the other seasons, was bitter." The allusion, of
course, is to the springtime of Bill's life, those eighteen years of childhood facetiously referred to as the
season of comfort in the novel's title but which the
French poet Rimbaud more aptly referred to as *"Une
Saison en Enfer"* in a title Vidal ironically echoes.

The Season of Comfort is usually read as a *roman
à clef*. Senator Hawkins is modeled on Vidal's grandfather; Charlotte is transparently Vidal's mother; Stephen Giraud and Robert Gilray are thinly disguised
versions of Vidal's father and stepfather; and Bill Giraud is clearly Vidal. But the novel offers none of the
spirited naughtiness and lively caricature of the true
roman à clef, only the longueurs of undigested autobiography masquerading as fiction. Specifically,
Vidal offers us a protagonist exempt from the sort of

faults attributed to the other characters, and, as if in self-pity, he offers us illustrations ad nauseam of the psychic damage done to the Vidal character by his mother. Narrative economy and psychological probability both dictate that Bill should respond more aggressively to his mother, and Vidal's failure to give us such scenes seems to spring from a fidelity to his personal memories rather than to his writerly good sense. *The Season of Comfort* seems therefore an autobiographical self-indulgence rather than a serious *roman à clef*.[2] One suspects Vidal of simply venting a grudge.

Yet *The Season of Comfort* is interesting for its stylistics. Even though they are generally unsuccessful, they show Vidal breaking away from the hard-boiled manner of his early Hemingway style, in search of a more experimental style. The early chapters, for instance, attempt a stream-of-consciousness effect, with elaborately triggered flashbacks and long passages of third-person narration which might as readily be in the first person, so closely do they follow the mental processes of individual characters. The penultimate chapter even attempts to represent simultaneous monologues on facing pages, with the verso pages belonging to Bill, the recto pages to Charlotte. The gimmick is appropriate to the alienation between Bill and his mother at that point in the story, but it is too clumsy a device to be accounted successful.

The most damaging of Vidal's stylistic experiments in *The Season of Comfort* are his experiments in tone. He strives for an arch tone early in the novel by employing a great many clichés in the stream-of-consciousness passages, thus making the point that his characters think in clichés, but belaboring the point. In his use of transitional and linking devices Vidal tries too hard to be clever, as in the single

broken sentence that attempts to span Chapters 5
and 6, and as in the white dress that Charlotte wears
to Bill's christening, an ex post facto vehicle for an
elaborate flashback involving another white dress.
Yet archness of tone and elegant transitional devices
are hallmarks of the mature Vidal style. *The Season
of Comfort* should therefore be understood as a transitional novel, marking the end of Vidal's use of the
Hemingway style and marking a serious attempt to
devise a voice of his own.

A Search for the King (1950) is a very different
sort of book, set in the twelfth century and recount-
ing the tale of Blondel de Néel, a French troubadour
alleged to have been a friend of Richard Coeur de
Lion. Legend has had it since the thirteenth century
that Blondel set out to find his king after Richard was
imprisoned by the Austrian duke Leopold as he
crossed Austria on his return from Palestine in 1192.
Blondel discovers where Richard is imprisoned by
sitting under a window of a certain castle in Austria
and singing a song that he and the king had composed together. Halfway through the song he pauses,
and Richard takes up the other half of the song, ena-
bling Blondel to return to England and report where
the king is being held.

Vidal uses this legend as his basic story line in *A
Search for the King,* and he embellishes it freely. In
the first section of the novel we are treated not only
to accounts of Richard's attempt to cross Austria and
of his eventual capture but also to an account of his
battle with a toothy green dragon. In the second
section Blondel's journey in quest of his liege is enriched with werewolves lurking in a dark forest, a
giant who speaks Latin and eats shepherd boys, and
a wonderfully macabre vampire who presides over a
spooky wood. The third section recounts Blondel's

discovery of Richard's prison and his journey back to England to report to the Queen Mother and also his disingenuous conversation with a wayfaring monk and his sweet dalliance with a German youth named Karl. The final section deals primarily with Richard's defeat of the usurper Prince John when their armies meet in the fields outside Nottingham. Robin Hood and his band put in a cameo appearance.

Because *A Search for the King* is Vidal's first novel in a historical mode, it must be seen as another experimental work, a giant step away from the Hemingway manner. But there is much about the novel that suggests a mature achievement. Its prose style is assured, its narrative pace is brisk, and its characterizations are lucid. Vidal displays no taste for the trumpery ornament or the quaintly period language that vitiates so much historical fiction, and he does not even poke fun at the medieval world in the way we might expect. The werewolves, vampires, and giants in the novel are taken seriously, although their treatment has just the right latitude to accommodate a modern understanding of how such folk beliefs developed. Vidal's werewolves are essentially highwaymen dressed in wolfskins who merely call themselves werewolves, exploiting the popular belief in such creatures. Similarly, Vidal's characters are credited with an entirely realistic sense of their world. Richard speaks about the Crusades in terms of trade routes, strategic positions, and loot rather than in terms of regaining the Holy Land for Christendom, and Blondel is entirely aware that he is turning into a legend through the agency of Karl's naïve and worshipful eyes.

If the historicity of *A Search for the King* points toward the great historical novels of Vidal's maturity, this straightforwardness in the novel seems to point backward to the unadorned realism of *The City and*

the Pillar. As a result, the novel seems to many to be
inexplicably positioned in the *oeuvre,* more contrary
to the general lines of Vidal's development than otherwise.[3] I prefer to emphasize the relevance that *A
Search for the King* has to the *oeuvre.* Specifically,
the motif of the two males, one of whom grounds his
existence in the other, is as fundamental to this novel
as it is to such novels as *The City and the Pillar,
Washington, D.C.,* and *Burr.* In fact, Vidal never renders the motif more affectingly. When Blondel finds
himself without a center and the world itself without
a center point after Richard's capture, his disorienta-
tion echoes our romantic impression that the medieval world enjoyed a centricity that we have lost. We
share profoundly in Blondel's heartache, as a result,
and it is tempting to use our understanding of the
two male figures in this novel to gloss all such pairs
in Vidal's fiction, although Vidal never again depicts
the relationship between two men in quite so charming (and asexual) a manner.

Dark Green, Bright Red (1950, revised 1968)
emerged out of Vidal's experience of living in
Guatemala in the late 1940s. Set in an unnamed Central American country, it is the story of an abortive
revolution waged by General Jorge Alvarez Asturias,
a former president of the republic who has recently
returned to the country after several years in New
Orleans, where he had lived in exile after the overthrow of his government. A motley crew of conspirators assists the general in his revolution: José Alvarez,
his playboy son, who delights in playing soldier;
Peter Nelson, an American who signs on as a mercenary; Charles de Cluny, a sometime French novelist
who serves as the general's speech writer; and Father Miguel, an ambitious priest. The general's
daughter Elena hangs about the conspirators, dream-

ing of her social life in New Orleans and sleeping
with Peter Nelson when her brother's eyes are elsewhere. Colonels Rojas and Aranhas seem to be the
general's flunkies, but they are actually traitors; Rojas
is in league with a United States fruit company that
really controls the country, and Aranhas is in league
with the government currently in power.

After describing the conspirators' establishment
of their headquarters and their attempts to turn the
native Indians into an organized army, Vidal describes their taking the towns of Nadatenango and
Tenango, the first bloodily, the second without a
shot. But in Tenango the general realizes that his
army is rapidly deserting and that Rojas has seized
the presidency of the republic through a plot more
subtle than his own, and so he and the other conspirators decamp. Their escape routes have long been in
readiness, and they leave behind only Father Miguel
and the dark green and bright red colorscape of the
tropical carnage. "Now the thing is done," Peter Nelson reflects cynically at the end. "The ambitious man
has fallen. Money rules."

Like *A Search for the King*, *Dark Green, Bright
Red* is an experimental work in which Vidal tests the
ability of a minor genre to accommodate his interests
and voice. Specifically, he experiments with the
novel of tropical intrigue, as developed by Joseph
Conrad and Graham Greene. Like those earlier novelists, Vidal dilutes the elements of adventure in his
narrative with monologic passages that are weary in
tone, and those passages turn what might have been
a simple tale of adventure into a study in *Weltschmerz*. The novel fails to engage the reader in its
weary mood, however. Peter Nelson, whose eyes
control what we see in the novel, has the curious
ability to turn dark green and bright red into mono-
tonal drab, and Nelson is himself utterly without col-

or. We never know why he was court-martialed by
the United States Army, for instance, and we never
glimpse any feeling in him for Elena or for his friend
José. His *Weltschmerz*, therefore, seems simple dull-
ness, a world-weariness born not of jadedness but of
disengagement. Many of Vidal's novels show a
marked inability to create rounded characters, but
this inability is never more damaging than it is in
Dark Green, Bright Red, for the novel has no psychological interest whatsoever.

Yet the novel offers some elementary political
and economic interest, as if in lieu of psychological
depth. Its title emblazons the trademark colors of the
United Fruit Company with obvious point, and the
prime backer of the revolution is the director of the
local fruit company, Mr. *Green;* Colonel Rojas (Spanish for "red") is Green's puppet. The manipulation of
Central American politics by such companies as
United Fruit is clearly indicated, then, but that
manipulation constitutes so minor an emphasis in the
novel that its focusing in the title seems a misemphasis.[4] Indeed, the real political and economic problem
focused by the novel is human selfishness, for the
characters from the general to the lowest Indian re-
cruit are motivationally long on gratification and
short on altruism, and even Peter Nelson maintains
that he involves himself in the revolution simply for
money. And yet we do not really believe Peter when
he says, "Money rules," for his *Weltschmerz* seems to
indicate a longing for peace rather than lucre. But
why is he a mercenary? *Dark Green, Bright Red* is
hopelessly at odds with itself in this regard. Peter's
tedious and ungrounded *Weltschmerz* has no vital
relation to the novel's political and economic cynicism, and his flatness as a character has no discernible
relation to the novel's vivid political palette.

* * *

Messiah (1954, revised 1965) is the first of Vidal's
novels to affect the guise of a written testament. Its
putative author is a very old man named Eugene
Luther (his names are Vidal's actual forenames), who
is living in the year 2000 and slowly dying in the
Egyptian town of Luxor. Luther spends his last days
writing about the origins and early days of the Cavite
movement, a messianic cult that he had helped to
launch in the 1950s, and the novel consists entirely
of the text of his written memoir and some diaristic
passages with which he annotates his text. The anno-
tations have their own present-day story; they make
clear that Luther has lived incognito in Egypt since
he fell out with the original leaders of Cavism in the
early days of the movement and that he fears for his
life inasmuch as the cult now tyrannizes all but a few
countries like Egypt. When two Cavite missionaries
check into Luther's hotel, he even suspects that they
have come to assassinate him until he discovers that
present-day cultists consider him apocryphal and
have expunged his name from their official histories.

The memoir begins on a summer afternoon in
the early 1950s, when Luther is invited to lunch by
Clarissa Lessing, his neighbor in the Hudson River
Valley, and is introduced to her young friend Iris
Mortimer. Iris tells Luther about John Cave, a morti-
cian's assistant from Seattle who has begun to preach
on the subject of death. Death is literally nothing,
Cave says, and therefore it should be thought of as a
boon. The idea is far from original, Luther knows, but
Cave is a spellbinder. Since Luther is half in love with
Iris, he allows Clarissa and Iris to draw him into the
small circle of Cave's intimates. Under the promotional drive of Paul Himmell, a Hollywood publicist,
that circle gives birth to Cavite, Inc., complete with
a board of directors, stockholders, and weekly television programs. The success of the company is phe-

nomenal, and Luther is even persuaded to ghost-
write "Cavesword," the body of Cavite scripture.

As Cave's doctrine of death becomes popular,
however, suicide (or "Cavesway") becomes wide-
spread; in a bid to displace Cave as leader of the cult,
Himmell insists that Cave set an example and commit Cavesway himself. Cave refuses, and he is supported by Iris and Luther. Cave is then killed by
Himmell's assassin, but Iris wrests control of the cult,
and Luther goes into hiding in Egypt. Cavism goes
on to become very nearly a universal religion under
Iris's governance, but it ceases to have much relationship to the eminently simple ideas of its morti-
cian founder.

Messiah is to a limited extent a parody of Christianity. As Luther remarks, Cave has a "pair of initials
calculated to amaze the innocent," and when Clarissa learns of Himmell's plot to do away with Cave, she
observes:

Where else could it lead? The same thing happened to
Jesus, you know. They kept pushing him to claim the king-
dom. Finally, they pushed too hard and he was killed. It
was the killing which perpetuated the legend.

The parallels between Cavism and Christianity
are clear enough. As Cave's promoter, Paul Himmell
plays the role of the apostle Paul, and Iris Mortimer
corresponds to the Virgin Mary, inspiring her own
cult after Cave's death; she is even considered to
have been Cave's mother in one of the flightier
schools of Cavite theology. Luther, of course, is one
of the evangelists—Luke, presumably—until he protests the errors of the cult and becomes Martin Luther. Specific correspondences between Cave's life
and the life of Christ are relatively few, however, for
Vidal's emphasis is not on the credentials that establish messiahship but on the merchandising tech-

niques that establish a religious empire atop Cave's modest talent. Thus, he draws our attention to the enormous organizational work that surrounds Cave, to the wholesale takeover of elements in the religions Cavism displaces, and to the distortion of Cave's simple creed when it must develop a coherency and a symbolism adequate for the ages. With some daring, he depicts Clarissa Lessing as a woman who transcends time, convincing us that she has been a contemporary of Christ as well as of Cave; through her ancient eyes, we understand that the world has always merchandised its messiahs. Vidal is so attentive to the merchandising process, in fact, that the evocation of the Christian myth seems incidental and generally innocent of blasphemous intent. As a result, what might have been a broad, sophomoric parody is a sharply focused novel of ideas.

In many ways, *Messiah* marks Vidal's coming into his own as a writer, for it seems to be the novel in which he developed the formula of his most successful fiction. Specifically, it was in *Messiah* that Vidal explored the possibilities of the fictive memoir and discovered that it is a genre which perfectly accommodates his sudden flashes of wit, his interest in revisionist ideas, and his occasional taste for a recherché syntax. At the same time, he no doubt discovered that the fictive memoir requires little in terms of character and plot development, those typical failings of his art. As I have argued, Vidal's gift has always been for the quick effect rather than for sustained development, and because the form of the memoir is so amenable to discontinuous effects, Vidal's voice seems more assured and more wholly his own in *Messiah* than ever before. It is as if the tendency to a grandiose rhetoric that Vidal has said he fears in himself[5] were kept at bay by the intimacy of the memoir form, as it was earlier by the Hemingway manner. It is as if Vidal were able to expose himself full voice only under the pretense that he speaks sotto voce.

Vidal's minor works include seven short stories. Six of them were written in the late 1940s and early 1950s, published variously, and collected under the title *A Thirsty Evil* (1956). "Pages from an Abandoned Journal" was written somewhat later, expressly for the publication of *A Thirsty Evil*. "The audience for the short story so shrank in my lifetime," Vidal has said, "that it would have taken a dedication of the sort I lacked to keep on."[6] The short stories were seminal in Vidal's development as a writer, however, because they developed his feel for first-person narration, and Vidal's best work is all in the first-person mode.

"Three Stratagems," in fact, employs *two* narrators. The first part of the story is narrated by a young prostitute named Michael, and the second and third parts by an aging widower named George Royal, who picks up Michael one day on the beach at Key West. Michael is quietly contemptuous of George's age and declining health, and he remarks confidently on his ability to seduce such men as George, "the ones with loose dimpled figures and bad teeth." But in the later sections of the story we hear George's version of the pickup, and his stratagems are ironically the equal of Michael's. This irony is compounded when Michael suffers an epileptic seizure in the course of the evening, for his contempt for dimpled figures and bad teeth is thereby rendered moot. With a coolness that makes Michael's confidence in his youth seem jejune, George looks on amusedly while Michael takes up the next day with another old man, for Michael is apparently unaware that the man is penniless and that he has met his match once again.

"Three Stratagems" is a wonderfully neat and effi-
cient story, sharp and effective in its plotting and
understated in its theme. The device of the double
narrator is the obvious key to its success.

"The Robin" is a slighter tale and not nearly so
successful in its mode of narration. It begins promis-
ingly with a sardonic narrator who describes how he
and his friend Oliver took pleasure in all sorts of
unpleasantness when they were nine years old. Au-
tomobile accidents were a source of great delight, he
says, matched only by other people's fights and the
gory splendors of a peep show. But when the boys
discover an injured robin one day, they fail to measure up as sadists, for they burst into tears after clum-
sily dispatching the bird. The narrator's tone
unfortunately shifts as abruptly as the boys' psycholo-
gy, and the shift to a sentimental point of view undercuts a number of passages in which childhood is seen
with a nicely disillusioned eye. The story seems trivial and emotionally false as a consequence, as inept a
tale as Vidal has ever told.

Like "The Robin," "A Moment of Green Laurel"
is a first-person story which looks back on childhood,
but it succeeds where the earlier story fails. The narrator is a young man who has returned to Washington after World War II. He walks out to his childhood
home in Rock Creek Park, and there he meets a
twelve-year-old boy who is gathering laurel to weave
into Roman wreaths, just as the narrator had done a
dozen years before. The correspondences between
the man and the boy quickly multiply: The boy lives
with his grandfather, he likes to read in the attic
library of the house, and his mother calls him to sup-
per with the narrator's own name. The man has
stumbled upon the ghost of his own childhood, we
understand, and there are many suggestions that the
man and his youthful *Doppelgänger* are Vidal him-

self. The story is as nostalgically sentimental as "The Robin," but its sentiment rings truer because the tone of the narration is consistently dreamlike and remote and because the narrator's responses are artfully blunted, as if wrapped in the cotton wool of sleep.

"The Zenner Trophy" is another story about homosexuality, narrated from the point of view of Mr. Beckman, a teacher in a New England preparatory school. Beckman is given the uncongenial task of expelling the school's top athlete because he was caught *in flagrante delicto* with another boy, and the expulsion is particularly awkward inasmuch as it has already been announced that the boy is to receive the Zenner trophy for clean sportsmanship at his graduation ceremony one week later. To Beckman's surprise, the boy is not in the least ashamed of his homosexual activity, only annoyed that the school has chosen to worry his parents with it. The boy's ability to take the reins of his life in hand wins the teacher's respect, for Beckman is not even able to take in hand the reins of their conversation. The story is interesting enough so far as it goes, but the boy's quiet confidence and the teacher's diffidence are simplistic, and the shock value they had in 1950 is no longer able to compensate for the lack of psychological depth in the story.

The narrator of "Erlinda and Mr. Coffin" is an impoverished Southern gentlewoman who rents one of the rooms in her Key West home to the title characters. The narrator thinks that Erlinda is Coffin's eight-year-old ward, but she is really a forty-one-year-old black dwarf and Coffin's wife. The narrator's mistake becomes manifest when Erlinda sets fire to the wife of the local shrimp magnate, enraged because the woman had refused her the starring role in an amateur production of *Camille*. The tale is rather

giddily contrived, and it can hardly be taken seriously as a work of art, but its histrionics are fun, and the
voice of the gentlewoman is carried off with panache.

"Pages from an Abandoned Journal" is a more
serious story. Its narrator is a failed Ph.D. candidate
who attends a party on the rue du Bac in Paris and
finds himself introduced to a world of homosexuality
and drugs presided over by one Elliott Magren, a
character Vidal bases on the extraordinary Denham
Fouts,[7] once known in the homosexual demimonde
as "The Best Kept Boy in the World." A series of
entries selected from the narrator's journal tell the
story of his growing involvement with Magren and
other homosexuals and of his lessening involvement
with women. Buried in the entries is his predictable
emergence as a homosexual—predictable because
the style of his journal is replete with gushing syntax
and ostentatious ellipses. The world of Elliott Magren, on the other hand, is replete with prostitution,
opium addiction, and the *gendarmerie*, and because
Magren's world contrasts so invidiously with the narrator's, the latter earns no points for merely discovering himself to be homosexual. It is a curious story,
filled with contempt for the effeminate sort of homosexual and best understood, perhaps, as Vidal's antidote to the pieties of "The Zenner Trophy."

"The Ladies in the Library" is the last story in *A
Thirsty Evil*—appropriately, a death story. Walter
Bragnet, a middle-aged writer, and his cousin Sybil
are the last remaining members of the Bragnet family, and they spend a sentimental weekend at the old
family home in Virginia, the house now owned by a
Miss Mortimer. Three childhood friends, the Parker
sisters, are invited to lunch, and Walter overhears
them argue about his death as they work at their
knitting in the library. As soon as they agree that he

is to die from a heart attack, one sister cuts the knot in her yarn, and Walter is suddenly conscious of a massive constriction in his chest. He sees Miss Mortimer smiling at him, "a familiar darkness in her lovely eyes." Death itself inhabits the house of Bragnet, in other words, while the Three Fates conspire in the library. The story works surprisingly well, given the difficulty of domesticating allegorical figures. The third-person viewpoint of the story allows us just the right degree of access into Walter's mind to pull off the allegorical stunt, and the tone of the story is pitched exactly right, neither offensively cute nor darkly mysterious. Vidal is obviously very skilled at this sort of fantasy, as "A Moment of Green Laurel" and *A Search for the King* bear out. One regrets that he has not written more stories in the mode.

Under the name Edgar Box, Vidal has also written three detective novels. *Death in the Fifth Position* (1952) deals with a series of murders that strike a ballet troupe at the same time that a United Veterans Committee is accusing the troupe of sheltering a communist. Peter Cutler Sargeant II, a young public relations agent, is called upon to deal with the problem, and he cleverly discovers the murderer. In *Death Before Bedtime* (1953) Sargeant is asked to assist Senator Leander Rhodes in his coming bid for the Presidency; when the senator is killed by a bomb that detonates in his study, Sargeant more consciously turns sleuth. In *Death Likes It Hot* (1954) Sargeant is the press agent for a society woman and is hired to elevate her social status from matron to dowager. When her niece drowns under mysterious circumstances at her Easthampton estate, her bid for greater social standing is compromised, and Sargeant has to unmask a killer once again.

The novels are enlivened considerably by Sar-

geant's urbane manner and observant eye, and the
worlds of ballet, politics, and the Social Register are
nicely impaled en route to the solution of the crimes.
Indeed, the novels are comedies of manners as much
as detective stories, and they are specifically comedies of sexual manners, for men and women are
forever pressing their knees against Peter Sargeant's
knees or baldly propositioning him in his bath. Peter's difficulties in fending off a Russian homosexual
with a lightning grope and in holding at bay the
committeewoman of a national political party are
particularly entertaining.

But the novels are no more than divertissements
of this order. Their plotting is adequate but more full
of loose ends than is proper in detective fiction, their
characterization is thin and full of gimmickry, and
even their best effects are slapdash. Vidal frankly
confesses that the novels are potboilers, written in
haste at a time when he desperately needed money.[8]
His cavalier attitude toward the novels is evident in
the blurb he supplied for the covers of 1964 paper-
back editions: "The work that Dr. Kinsey began with
statistics, Edgar Box has completed with wit in the
mystery novel—Gore Vidal."

In the mid-1950s Vidal also wrote a great many
television scripts (nearly a hundred by his estima-
tion), and in succeeding years he wrote the scripts for
some dozen Hollywood films and seven full-length
plays. A fair measure of success and recognition ac-
crued from this outpouring. The play *Visit to a Small
Planet* enjoyed considerable success on the television
screen in May 1955, and in an expanded version it
enjoyed a long run on Broadway in 1957, followed by
a successful run in Europe and a respectable adaptation on film. *The Best Man* (1960) also enjoyed a successful run on Broadway, and Vidal's script for the

film version of the play was generally considered one of the best of its year. Vidal's remarks on his dramatic works have not encouraged us to take them seriously, however:

I must confess right off that I am not at heart a playwright. I am a novelist turned temporary adventurer; and I chose to write television, movies, plays for much the same reason that Captain Morgan selected the Spanish Main for his peculiar . . . and not dissimilar . . . sphere of operations.[9]

I am inclined to take Vidal at his self-denigrating word. Although all the scripts available to us are workmanlike, and almost all have fine moments, they tend to be marred by artistic and ideational compromises in deference to the enormous sums of money involved in their commercial production. These compromises are most evident in the endings of the full-length plays, which typically soften the cynicism of earlier acts and seem thereby to plead inoffensiveness ex post facto.

On the March to the Sea (1960) and *Romulus* (1962) are illustrative. The first is a Civil War play in which a man named John Hinks sends his sons off to battle and encourages his neighbors to set fire to their homes lest the Union troops make use of them, all in the name of an honor that he does not himself uphold. Hinks is a parvenu, a hypocrite, and an opportunist—everything that Vidal detests. Yet Vidal allows him an unlikely change of heart after one of his sons denounces him, and Vidal's cynicism becomes the cheapest melodrama when Hinks heroically fires his home at the end of the play while a Union officer murmurs voluptuously, "Fire . . . Oh, Hinks, how beautiful! I never thought you could do it."

Romulus, an adaptation of Friedrich Dürrenmatt's *Romulus der Grosse,* similarly betrays its cynicism. Romulus is the last of the Roman emperors and a sometime professor of history who attends to his chicken farm while Odoaker the Goth devastates his empire. Romulus deliberately fosters the end of the empire through his neglect, for his historical sense tells him that "Rome knew truth, but chose power ... knew humaneness, but chose tyranny ... debased herself as well as those she governed." Romulus even parries the efforts of an international businessman named Otto Rupf to save the empire, and so it is disconcerting when Romulus meets Odoaker at the end of the play, discovers that he too is a chicken fancier, and agrees with him upon a policy of mutual peace.

The Best Man (1960) and *Weekend* (1968) are both typical, election-year plays that suffer from the same problem. *The Best Man* is set at a nominating convention in Philadelphia at which William Russell and Joe Cantwell are rivals for their party's presidential endorsement. Russell is a witty and slightly arrogant intellectual who reminds one of Adlai Stevenson, and Cantwell is a mindless opportunist who evokes both Richard Nixon and Joseph McCarthy.[10] Each candidate considers mudslinging as a way of defeating his opponent. Cantwell, in fact, brings up Russell's history of mental breakdown, and Russell briefly considers smearing Cantwell with homosexuality. Ultimately, such invidiousness destroys the chances of both candidates, and the nomination goes to a political unknown, a thinly disguised Harry Truman. The political contest is short-circuited, and the Truman character functions as a crude *deus ex machina*.

In *Weekend*, a presidential candidate is at odds with his son over the son's engagement to a black woman, and the father and son consequently proceed to enlist the support of their respective generations and to engage in mutual blackmail. At the last moment, an improbable public opinion poll discovers that Americans would not object to a President with a black daughter-in-law, rendering the generational ugliness moot.

An Evening with Richard Nixon and ... (1972), another election-year offering, is a more experimental and aesthetically honest play. Its basic ploy is that the deceased Presidents Washington, Eisenhower, and Kennedy discuss President Nixon's life in something of a kangaroo court, while Nixon speaks for himself in words taken from his actual speeches, writings, and interviews. Nixon's words are carefully arranged to emphasize his penchant for contradicting himself, and Nixonian howlers are spread generously about. As if to dissipate this concentrated attack on Nixon, a disembodied voice asks at the end of the play, "Who cut down that cherry tree?" We understand the question to mean, "Who undercut America's integrity?" Kennedy quickly answers, "Nixon did," but Eisenhower, in his plodding, honest way, says, "Now we gotta be fair about that one. We . . . uh, we all did!" For once there is no *deux ex machina* to resolve the situation and absolve the play of its cynicism, but neither is there dramatic action to carry us along, and the play has not generally proven stageworthy.

The best of Vidal's plays is the early *Visit to a Small Planet* (1957), an engaging fantasy in which Kreton, a visitor from space, arrives in Virginia, hoping to view the Battle of Bull Run in 1861. Having arrived too late by almost a century, he becomes a houseguest of the Spelding family and the object of some concern to the federal government when he makes it clear that he intends to start World War III. His motives are sensuous rather than malicious, for he dotes on the primitive and violent emotions of

men and has made them his special study. Because
he can read minds and regularly attests to the violent
emotions of the other characters, the audience has no
choice but to accept his opinion that war is mankind's
finest art. But having carried his parody of our bel-
licose culture so far, Vidal typically pulls in the horns
of his cynicism. Before Kreton can work his will and
start a war, the ingenue summons another visitor
from space who reclaims Kreton and explains that he
is mentally and morally retarded, a child who es-
caped from his nursery. The use of a *deus ex machina*
succeeds better in *Visit to a Small Planet* than in
Vidal's other plays, however, because the tone of the
play is farcical throughout. Indeed, the point of the
play is precisely that our civilization is farcical in its
warmongering and mentally retarded in its love of
violence.

Vidal's minor writings are minor indeed if we
except *A Search for the King*, "A Moment of Green
Laurel," *Messiah*, and *Visit to a Small Planet*. But
even the obvious hackwork is covert testament to
Vidal's professionalism, to his willingness to meet the
exigencies of the marketplace so long as it sustains his
art. If television ephemera can finance the writing of
a *Julian*, after all, what loss? And as I have suggested,
the minor writings were the workshop in which
Vidal developed his mature aesthetic. His struggle
with plot is there, along with the emergence of his
verbal wit, the occasional experiment, and his discovery of the memoir's capaciousness. Workshops are
spurned only by those who consume art, not by those
who care for its being.

9
A Summary Assessment

Because Vidal is a writer with many voices, his career seems a history of elaborate feints and passes. His first novel, *Williwaw,* was hard-hitting in the best Hemingway tradition, but *The City and the Pillar* applied the Hemingway manner to a homosexual theme and delivered a limp-wristed uppercut to our expectations. A series of undistinguished novels in the 1950s convinced us that Vidal was one of those writers whose careers peak early, but 1964 served up *Julian,* an intimidating novel in terms of both scholarship and aesthetics. The trilogy *Washington, D.C., Burr,* and *1876* followed shortly in tandem with the Breckinridge confections, and once again Vidal proved difficult to categorize, for the trilogy is a formidable overview of American history, while the Breckinridge novels are the purest camp. *Kalki* disinterred the apocalyptic theme we had thought abandoned with *Messiah, Creation* disinterred *Julian*'s interest in ancient history, and *Two Sisters* came out of nowhere, its autobiographical dazzle wholly unexpected. Vidal's performance is nothing less than ventriloquistic.

Yet there are performances of which Vidal seems incapable. The formal discipline of modernism seems beyond him, for instance. Faithful instead to an eighteenth-century aesthetic of the novel, Vidal crams gossip, journalism, sociology, philosophy, history, and literary parody into a narrative hopper and christens the mix a novel in the name of the god Vitality. Also beyond him is the high-romantic pretense that interpersonal love is the ultimate adventure. A more traditional respect for self-love claims his allegiance, and all his major characters are estimable narcissists. Is Vidal a reactionary? Is he a classicist in his tastes and values, stepping back over the nineteenth century as over something unpleasant on the footpath? Is he a Petronius, as he has several times been labeled, casting a dispirited eye over the last days of the American empire?[1] Is his vaunted radicalism a radical traditionalism? Yes. And he plays that role, like his others, with panache.

Vidal is also a *farceur*, of course, and insouciance and insolence regularly join forces in his rhetoric. The seriousness of his reactionary stance is therefore open to question. It is entirely possible that his celebrated distaste for modernism and his fulminations against romantic love are simply apologias for the glaring incapacities of his fiction, a policy of attack or be attacked, as it were.[2] But apologias aside, the weakness of Vidal's larger structures and his general inability to make his characters come alive are *defining* incapacities of his fiction—importantly so, because they define him as an artist of the middle rank. A comparison with the visual arts will perhaps amplify this point. A draftsman of middling talent can often control his line in small scale and produce elegant drawings of aesthetic moment. But to work with the same élan on a grand scale is an achievement of the highest order and requires a much greater talent. Vidal is an artist of the middle rank primarily because his talent is for the small scale: for the anecdote, for the scene, ineluctably for the sentence.[3]

Pointing out this limitation in Vidal's art does not constitute an attack. Vidal's anecdotes and scenes are not so much line drawings as richly conceived impasto, clotted with intelligence, layered with wit, and worked to the substantiality of bas-relief. And Vidal's prose, as I have argued, is very fine. His deft touch with syntax, his marvelous ear for cadence, and his adroit sense of tone are entirely masterful. If even his best characters are not quite flesh and blood, they are, like Cleopatra, fire and air, and I fancy that Shakespeare's queen would have applauded Myra and wily old Burr, recognizing in their flights of imposture an artifice commensurate with her own.

The great charm of Vidal's writing is its auctorial audacity. The risqué, the demotic, and the left wing always threaten to bring down his elegant prose and mannered sophistication, and a devilish wit always counterpoints his angelically lucid style. It is a bravura performance withal, and in a sense Vidal is less a storyteller than a performer. His fictions do not tend to establish self-contained worlds independent of his mediation; rather, they constitute a juggler's feats, with Vidal compounding the most extraordinary materials not for the art of jugglery alone but for the opportunity to wear an audacious face. We are always aware of that face in Vidal's mature fictions. A quip, an outrageously sentimental *glissade*, an autobiographical indiscretion—all turn his jugglery into a performance, a *celebration* of auctorial selfhood. As I observed at the beginning of this study, Vidal's publicly crafted selves may not correspond to his private selves, but what matter? Selfhood is connoisseur's play in the novels, as stylish and entertaining a fiction as one could wish. The Vidalian persona, *con brio*, is the ultimate achievement of Vidal's art.

Notes

1. THE LIFE

1. Eve Auchincloss and Nancy Lynch, "Disturber of the Peace: Gore Vidal," *Mademoiselle*, September 1961, p. 179.
2. See especially Eugene Walter, "Conversations with Gore Vidal," *Transatlantic Review* 4 (Summer 1960), 5–17.
3. Anaïs Nin, *The Diary of Anaïs Nin, Volume IV, 1944–1947,* ed. Gunther Stuhlmann (New York: Harcourt, Brace, Jovanovich, 1971), pp. 106, 113, 121.
4. The novel is among the Vidal papers deposited with the State Historical Society of Wisconsin. The 175-page typescript is entitled "A Novel," and on the title page Vidal has written, "nearly finished—begun at Exeter '43—*abandoned.*"
5. Hollywood gives partial credit for the screenplay to Robert Hamer.
6. Gore Vidal, "The Subject Doesn't Object" [review of *Gore Vidal* by Ray Lewis White], *New York Times Book Review*, 1 September 1968, p. 19. Reprinted as "Gore Vidal" in Gore Vidal, *Homage to Daniel Shays* (New York: Random House, 1972), pp. 302–6.
7. Buckley's account of the episode was published under the title "On Experiencing Gore Vidal," *Esquire*, August 1969, pp. 108–13. Vidal responded in the September issue of *Esquire*, pp. 140–43.
8. Michael Segell, "The Highbrow Railings of Gore Vidal" [interview], *Rolling Stone*, 15 May 1980, p. 42.
9. Arthur Cooper, "Gore Vidal on . . . Gore Vidal" [interview], *Newsweek*, 18 November 1974, p. 98.

145

2. THE VIDALIAN MANNER: *The Judgment of Paris, Two Sisters, Kalki*

1. Gore Vidal, "Foreword," *Visit to a Small Planet and Other Television Plays* (Boston: Little, Brown, 1956), p. xv. Reprinted in Gore Vidal, *Homage to Daniel Shays* (New York: Random House, 1972), p. 30.
2. John W. Aldridge, "Three Tempted Him," *New York Times Book Review*, 9 March 1952, p. 4.
3. One of Vidal's remarks in the Mitzel and Abbott interview is relevant: "I think you will find it takes a long time to find your tone of voice. I didn't until *Judgment of Paris*. I published five or six books before I really got it. I wouldn't say I got it right, but I got it accurate." John Mitzel and Stephen Abbott, *Myra & Gore: A New View of Myra Breckinridge and a Candid Interview with Gore Vidal, A Book for Vidalophiles* (Dorchester, Mass.: Manifest Destiny Books, 1974), p. 78. The interview appeared originally in *Fag Rag*, Winter-Spring 1974, pp. 1, 3–9.
4. Nin's comments have been cited in Chapter 1. See Vidal's essay "The Fourth Diary of Anaïs Nin" in *Homage to Daniel Shays*, pp. 403–9, for Vidal's reaction to his appearance in Nin's diary.
5. "Jimmy" is probably James Tremble, to whom *The City and the Pillar* is dedicated. See below, Chapter 3, note 6.

3. THE EARLY SUCCESSES: *Williwaw, The City and the Pillar*

1. See, for instance, John Watson Aldridge's remarks in *After the Lost Generation* (New York: McGraw-Hill, 1951), pp. 170–1.
2. Willard strangles Ford in the unrevised version of the novel.
3. Leslie Fiedler has the classic discussion in his influential essay "Come Back to the Raft Ag'in, Huck Honey!" *Partisan Review* 15 (June 1948), 664–71, re-

printed in his *An End to Innocence* (Boston: Beacon Press, 1955), pp. 142–51.

4. Alfred C. Kinsey and his associates published *Sexual Behavior in the Human Male* (Philadelphia: W. B. Saunders) during the week of 24 January 1948; *The City and the Pillar* was published during the week of 10 January 1948. For a review of *The City and the Pillar* that reflects prepublication familiarity with the Kinsey Report, see Richard McLaughlin, "Precarious Status," *Saturday Review of Literature*, 10 January 1948, pp. 14–15. Vidal claims that Kinsey wrote to him after the novel's publication, congratulating him on his "work in the field."

5. For instances of moralizing removed from the text, see in the unrevised version Willard's reflection on malicious homosexuals, p. 105, and the cocktail party analysis of castrating women, pp. 236–40. *The City and the Pillar* (New York: E. P. Dutton, 1948).

6. One senses auctorial involvement in this rigidity. See Bernard Dick's study for an interesting speculation that James Tremble, to whom the novel is dedicated, was something of a Bob Ford character in Vidal's life. *The Apostate Angel* (New York: Random House, 1974), pp. 36–38. References to boyhood lovers who die in battle also occur in *The Season of Comfort* ("Jimmy Wesson"), "Pages from an Abandoned Journal" ("Jimmy"), *Washington, D.C.* ("Scotty"), and *Two Sisters* ("Jimmy").

4. THE ANCIENT WORLD: *Julian, Creation*

1. John Leonard, Review of *Creation*, *New York Times*, 10 March 1981, p. C9.

2. Gore Vidal, *Three by Gore Vidal* (New York: New American Library, 1962), p. 234.

3. Wilmer Cave Wright (trans.), *The Works of the Emperor Julian*, 3 vols., The Loeb Classical Library (New York: Macmillan, 1930).

4. Mary Renault, "The Wise Lord and the Lie," *New York Review of Books*, 14 May 1981, p. 30.

5. THE AMERICAN TRILOGY: *Washington, D.C., Burr, 1876*

1. Quoted in Robert J. Stanton and Gore Vidal, *Views from a Window: Conversations with Gore Vidal* (Secaucus, N.J.: Lyle Stuart, 1980), p. 257. The remark appeared originally in Beverly Kempton, "Conversations with Gore Vidal," *Oui*, April 1975.
2. Vidal first claimed that the three novels constitute a trilogy in 1976 upon the publication of *1876*. The classification is somewhat moot and certainly ex post facto, as Vidal did not envision a trilogy in 1967 when he published *Washington, D.C.* See Vidal's comments to Judy Halfpenny on the subject, quoted in Stanton, pp. 103–4, otherwise unpublished.
3. Stanton, p. 102.
4. Stanton, p. 102.
5. See above, Chapter 3, note 6.
6. John Lombardi suggests these parallels in "Bicentennial Gore," *Oui*, July 1976, pp. 31–32.
7. Peter Conrad first suggested that this logic was implicit in the novel. "Re-inventing America," *Times Literary Supplement*, 26 March 1976, pp. 347–8.
8. Vidal to Hollis Alpert: "That's why I wrote my American trilogy. . . . I wanted to tell myself the story of the history of the country because I found history as boring in school as everybody else did, and I knew the national story could not have been that dull, and it wasn't." Hollis Alpert, "Dialogue on Film: Gore Vidal," *American Film*, April 1977, p. 44. Reprinted in Stanton, p. 251.

6.   THE BRECKINRIDGE NOVELS

1. Susan Sontag, "Notes on 'Camp,'" *Against Interpretation and Other Essays* (New York: Farrar, Straus & Giroux, 1966), pp. 275–92.
2. Parker Tyler, *Magic and Myth of the Movies* (New York: Henry Holt, 1947). Tyler's analyses of Hollywood films are not generally understood as camp, but Tyler seemed to invite a camp understanding of his work when he wrote to *The New York Times* upon the release of the film *Myra Breckinridge,* "The purpose of my satiric-surreal film criticism, circa 1947 and later, was to make it with the literary quarterlies while enjoying myself." *New York Times,* 19 July 1970, p. B4.
3. MGM never issued a film entitled *Siren of Babylon,* but United Artists issued *Siren of Atlantis,* starring Maria Montez, in 1948 as part of a series of "Siren" pictures. As the "glamour" studio of the period, MGM is a more appropriate milieu for Myra than United Artists, however, and I presume that Vidal altered the title and studio for that reason.
4. Vidal is of the same opinion. In response to a 1977 query, he said, "I like *Myron* as much or more than *Myra* (naturally, *Myra* was the first creation and so unique). I think the invention in *Myron* was more interesting and the jokes wilder." Robert J. Stanton and Gore Vidal, *Views from a Window: Conversations with Gore Vidal* (Secaucus, N.J.: Lyle Stuart, 1980), p. 68.

7.   THE ESSAYS

1. See, for instance, Mitchell S. Ross, *The Literary Politicians* (Garden City, N.Y.: Doubleday, 1978), pp. 247–300. Vidal himself loathes his essays being preferred to his novels.
2. For Simon's own reaction to the satire, see John Simon, "The Good and Bad of Gore Vidal," *Esquire,*

August 1977, pp. 22–24, reprinted in John Simon, *Paradigms Lost: Reflections on Literacy and Its Decline* (New York: Clarkson N. Potter, 1980), pp. 105–10.

3. Michael S. Lasky, "Gore Vidal: His Writings," *Writer's Digest*, March 1975, p. 25.

8. THE MINOR WORKS

1. Gerald Clarke, "The Art of Fiction," *Paris Review* 15 (Fall 1974), 135. Reprinted as "Gore Vidal" in *Writers at Work: The Paris Review Interviews*, Fifth Series, ed. George Plimpton (New York: Penguin, 1981), p. 286. Reprinted also in Robert J. Stanton and Gore Vidal, *Views from a Window: Conversations with Gore Vidal* (Secaucus, N.J.: Lyle Stuart, 1980), p. 87.

2. Vidal to Ray Lewis White, 6 May 1966: *"The Season of Comfort* is autobiographical which explains why it so perfectly fails." Ray Lewis White, *Gore Vidal* (Boston: Twayne, 1968), p. 140.

3. See, for instance, John Watson Aldridge, *After the Lost Generation: A Critical Study of the Writers of Two Wars* (New York: McGraw-Hill, 1951), p. 182; and Mitchell S. Ross, *The Literary Politicians* (Garden City, N.Y.: Doubleday, 1978), p. 255.

4. Vidal told Judy Halfpenny in 1978 that he had failed in *Dark Green, Bright Red* "to bring into focus the theme." Stanton, p. 92, otherwise unpublished.

5. Clarke, p. 139, reprinted in *Writers at Work*, p. 290; reprinted also in Stanton, p. 63.

6. Stanton, p. 66.

7. Vidal to Judy Halfpenny, 1976: "I suppose I was grafting onto [Jim Willard] some characteristics of a marvelous Southern whore named Denham Foutts [*sic*], whom I describe in 'Pages from an Abandoned Journal.' " Stanton, p. 93, otherwise unpublished. Denham Fouts also figures in Speed Lamkin's *The Easter Egg*

Hunt, Christopher Isherwood's *Down There on a Visit,* and Truman Capote's novel in progress *Answered Prayers.*

8. Michael S. Lasky, "Gore Vidal: His Writings," *Writer's Digest,* March 1975, p. 26. The relevant passage is reprinted in Stanton, p. 93.

9. Gore Vidal, "Preface to the American Edition" [of *Visit to a Small Planet*], *Three Plays* (London: Heinemann, 1962), p. 253.

10. Vidal disagrees: "Contrary to rumor, I was not writing about Adlai Stevenson, Richard Nixon and Harry Truman. There were elements of these men in each of the characters, but no more." Gore Vidal, *Rocking the Boat* (Boston: Little, Brown, 1962), p. 300. In fairness to Vidal's point of view, it must be remarked that the casting of the play tended to emphasize the real-life equivalents of his characters and to cement the equations in the public mind. But see Vidal's essay "Politics, Washington, D.C.," *New Statesman,* 4 May 1973, pp. 639–40, reprinted as "Political Melodramas" in his *Matters of Fact and of Fiction (Essays 1973–1976)* (New York: Random House, 1977), pp. 259–64, which concedes that the "noble if waffling character in the play was based on Adlai Stevenson."

9. A SUMMARY ASSESSMENT

1. See especially Gerald Clarke, "Petronius Americanus: The Ways of Gore Vidal," *Atlantic,* March 1972, pp. 44–51.

2. See especially Vidal's essay "Love, Love, Love," *Partisan Review* 26 (Fall 1959), 613–20. Reprinted in Gore Vidal, *Homage to Daniel Shays* (New York: Random House, 1972), pp. 47–57.

3. Michael S. Lasky to Vidal: "Ultimately, how would you like to be remembered?" Vidal: "I suppose as the person who wrote the best sentences in his time." Michael S. Lasky, "Gore Vidal: His Writings," *Writer's*

Digest, March 1975, p. 26. Quoted in Robert J. Stanton and Gore Vidal, *Views from a Window: Conversations with Gore Vidal* (Secaucus, N.J.: Lyle Stuart, 1980), p. 53.

Bibliography

I. Works by Gore Vidal

Williwaw. New York: E. P. Dutton, 1946.
In a Yellow Wood. New York: E. P. Dutton, 1947.
The City and the Pillar. New York: E. P. Dutton: 1948.
   Rev. ed., New York: E. P. Dutton, 1965.
The Season of Comfort. New York: E. P. Dutton, 1949.
Dark Green, Bright Red. New York: E. P. Dutton, 1950.
   Rev. ed., New York: New American Library, 1968.
A Search for the King: A Twelfth-Century Legend. New
   York: E. P. Dutton, 1950.
Death in the Fifth Position [Edgar Box, pseud.]. New York:
   E. P. Dutton, 1952.
The Judgment of Paris. New York: E. P. Dutton, 1952. Rev.
   ed., Boston: Little, Brown, 1965.
Death Before Bedtime [Edgar Box, pseud.]. New York: E.
   P. Dutton, 1953.
Death Likes It Hot [Edgar Box, pseud.]. New York: E. P.
   Dutton, 1954.
Messiah. New York: E. P. Dutton, 1954. Rev. ed., Boston:
   Little, Brown, 1965.
A Thirsty Evil: Seven Short Stories. New York: Zero Press,
   1956.
Visit to a Small Planet and Other Television Plays. Boston:
   Little, Brown, 1956.
Visit to a Small Planet: A Comedy Akin to Vaudeville
   [Broadway version]. Boston: Little, Brown, 1957.
The Best Man: A Play about Politics. Boston: Little, Brown,
   1960.
On the March to the Sea: A Southron Tragedy. Evergreen
   Playscript Series. New York: Grove Press, n.d.

153

Rocking the Boat. Boston: Little, Brown, 1962.

Romulus: A New Comedy, Adapted from a Play by Friedrich Dürrenmatt. New York: Dramatists Play Service, 1962.

Three: Williwaw, A Thirsty Evil, Julian the Apostate. New York: New American Library, 1962.

Three Plays. London: William Heinemann, 1962. [Contents: *Visit to a Small Planet, On the March to the Sea, The Best Man,* "Love, Love, Love: An Essay."]

Julian: A Novel. Boston: Little, Brown, 1964.

Washington, D.C.: A Novel. Boston: Little, Brown, 1967.

Myra Breckinridge. Boston: Little, Brown, 1968.

Sex, Death and Money. New York: Bantam Books, 1968.

Weekend: A Comedy in Two Acts. New York: Dramatists Play Service, 1968.

Reflections Upon a Sinking Ship. Boston: Little, Brown, 1969.

Two Sisters: A Memoir in the Form of a Novel. Boston: Little, Brown, 1970.

An Evening with Richard Nixon. New York: Random House, 1972.

Homage to Daniel Shays: Collected Essays 1952–1972. New York: Random House, 1972.

Burr: A Novel. New York: Random House, 1973.

Myron: A Novel. New York: Random House, 1974.

1876: A Novel. New York: Random House, 1976.

Matters of Fact and of Fiction (Essays 1973–1976). New York: Random House, 1977.

Kalki: A Novel. New York: Random House, 1978.

Gore Vidal. New York: William Heinemann, 1979. [Contents: *Julian, Williwaw, The Judgment of Paris, Messiah, The City and the Pillar.*]

Creation: A Novel. New York: Random House, 1981.

II. WORKS ABOUT GORE VIDAL

Books

Dick, Bernard F. *The Apostate Angel: A Critical Study of Gore Vidal.* New York: Random House, 1974.

Mitzel, John, and Steven Abbott. *Myra & Gore: A New*

View of Myra Breckinridge and a Candid Interview with Gore Vidal, A Book for Vidalophiles. Dorchester, Mass.: Manifest Destiny Books, 1974.

Stanton, Robert J. *Gore Vidal: A Primary and Secondary Bibliography*. Boston: G. K. Hall, 1978.

Stanton, Robert J., and Gore Vidal. *Views from a Window: Conversations with Gore Vidal*. Secaucus, N.J.: Lyle Stuart, 1980.

White, Ray Lewis. *Gore Vidal*. Twayne's United States Authors Series, 135. Boston: Twayne, 1968.

Interviews with Vidal

Aronson, Steven M. L. "Gore Vidal: Creation," *Interview*, May 1981, pp. 46–50.

Auchincloss, Eve, and Nancy Lynch. "Disturber of the Peace: Gore Vidal," *Mademoiselle*, September 1961, pp. 132–3, 176–9.

Clarke, Gerald. "The Art of Fiction," *Paris Review* 15 (Fall 1974), 130–65. Reprinted in *Writers at Work: The Paris Review Interviews*, Fifth Series. Ed. George Plimpton. New York: Penguin, 1981, pp. 283–311.

——————. "Petronius Americanus: The Ways of Gore Vidal," *Atlantic*, March 1972, pp. 44–51.

Kempton, Beverly. "Conversations with Gore Vidal," *Oui*, April 1975, p. 72.

Lasky, Michael S. "The Complete Works on Gore Vidal: His Workings," *Writer's Digest*, March 1975, pp. 20–26.

Segell, Michael. "The Highbrow Railings of Gore Vidal," *Rolling Stone*, 15 May 1980, pp. 40–43.

Walter, Eugene. "Conversations with Gore Vidal," *Transatlantic Review* 4 (Summer 1960), 5–17.

Essays and Reviews

Aldridge, John Watson. "Gore Vidal: The Search for a King," *After the Lost Generation: A Critical Study of the Writers of the Two Wars*. New York: McGraw-Hill, 1951, pp. 170–83.

Allen, Walter. "The Last Pagan," *New York Review of Books*, 30 July 1964, pp. 20–21.

Boyette, Purvis E. " 'Myra Breckinridge' and Imitative Form," *Modern Fiction Studies* 17 (Summer 1971), 229–38.

Buckley, William F., Jr. "On Experiencing Gore Vidal,"
    Esquire, August 1969, pp. 108–13. Reprinted in *Smil-
    ing Through the Apocalypse: Esquire's History of the
    Sixties*. Ed. Harold Hayes. New York: McCall Publish-
    ing, 1970, pp. 911–46.

Conrad, Peter. "Hall of Mirrors: The Novels of Gore Vid-
    al," London *Sunday Times*, 27 March 1977, p. 35.

————. "Look at Us," *New Review* 2 (July 1975), 63–66.

————. "Re-inventing America," *Times Literary Supple-
    ment*, 26 March 1976, pp. 347–8.

Epstein, Joseph. "What Makes Vidal Run," *Commentary*
    63 (June 1977), 72–75.

Krim, Seymour. "Reflections on a Ship That's Not Sinking
    at All," *London Magazine*, May 1970, pp. 26–43.

Mitzel, John, et al. "Some Notes on Myra B," *Fag Rag*, Fall
    1973, pp. 21–5.

Nin, Anaïs. *The Diary of Anaïs Nin. Volume IV, 1944–
    1947*. Ed. Gunther Stuhlmann. New York: Harcourt,
    Brace, Jovanovich, 1971, pp. 106, 113, 121.

Pritchett, V. S. "How to Say Serious Things," *New York
    Review of Books*, 26 May 1977, pp. 8–9.

Ross, Mitchell S. "Gore Vidal," *The Literary Politicians*.
    Garden City, N.Y.: Doubleday, 1978, pp. 247–300.

Simon, John. "The Good and Bad of Gore Vidal," *Esquire*,
    August 1977, pp. 22–24. Reprinted in John Simon,
    Paradigms Lost. New York: Clarkson N. Potter, 1980,
    pp. 105–10.

Spender, Stephen. "Gore Vidal, Essayist," *New York Times
    Book Review*, 17 April 1977, p. 1.

————. "Private Eye," *New York Review of Books*, 22
    March 1973, pp. 6–8.

Wilhelm, John F., and Mary Ann Wilhelm. " 'Myra Breck-
    inridge': A Study of Identity," *Journal of Popular Cul-
    ture* 3 (Winter 1969), 590–9.

Wood, Michael. "Passions in Politics," *New York Review of
    Books*, 29 April 1976, pp. 30–31.

Ziolkowski, Theodore. *Fictional Transfigurations of Jesus*.
    Princeton, N.J.: Princeton University Press, 1972, pp.
    250–7.

Index

Adams, Henry, 10, 77, 91
Adler, Renata, 30
Agnew, Spiro, 116
Aldridge, John W., 13
Allyson, June, 97
"American Plastic: The Matter of Fiction," 110, 113
Anderson, Sherwood, 39
Astor, Mr. and Mrs. William, 86, 90
Auchincloss, Hugh D. (stepfather), 2, 72, 84
Aumont, Jean Pierre, 104
Austen, Howard, 8

"Barn Burning" (Faulkner), television adaptation by Vidal, 6
Barth, John, 113
Barthelme, Donald, 113
Ben Hur (film scenario), Vidal as collaborator on, 6
Best Man, The (play), 6, 137, 139
bigotry, 69–70
Bowen, Eliza, 77, 79, 81
Bowles, Paul, 5
Box, Edgar (pseudonym), 5, 136
Boyer, Charles, 104
Bryant, William Cullen, 82, 86, 87
Buckley, William F., Jr., 7, 117
Burr, 8, 45, 75–85
  critique of, 77–78, 84–85
  and daughter Theodosia, 77
  historical characters in, 76, 80
  historicity of, 77–78
  iconoclasm of, 76–80
  language of, 82–83
Burr, Aaron, 73, 75–84, 91, 92

Caligula (screenplay), 9
"Calvino's Novels," 112
camp literature, 96
Capote, Truman, 114
Catered Affair, The (screenplay), 6
Chase Manhattan Bank, 111
Chayefsky, Paddy, 6
Christianity, 47, 48, 52, 54, 130–31
Christie, Agatha, 15

CIA (Central Intelligence
    Agency), 26
City and the Pillar, The, 4,
    5, 8, 37–44
  critique of, 42–44
  homosexual theme of,
    37–44
  identity crisis in, 42
  revision of, 37, 38, 43
  similarity to other novels
    in, 39–40
Confucius, 64
Conkling, Roscoe, 90
Conrad, Joseph, 127
Cornfeld, Bernard, 111
Corydon (Gide), 5
Crawford, Joan, 113
Creation, 8, 45, 58–66
  critique of, 61–62
  Confucian portrayal in,
    64–65
  Greek civilization por-
    trayed in, 62–63, 66
  historicity in, 58, 60–62,
    65
  nonfictional characters
    of, 59, 62, 64, 66
  Persian-Greek wars and,
    58–59
  religious elements in, 60,
    62–65
critique, 142–44
  of the American trilogy,
    92–93
  of *Burr*, 77–78, 84–85
  of *The City and the Pil-
    lar*, 42–44
  of *Creation*, 61–62, 65–66
  of *Dark Green, Bright
    Red*, 127–28
  of *1876*, 91–93

of essays by Vidal, 112–
    14, 116–17
  of *The Judgment of Paris*,
    13–14
  of *Julian*, 49–51, 58
  of *Kalki*, 26–31
  of *Myra Breckinridge*, 94,
    100, 108–09
  of *Myron*, 102–03, 106
  of *The Season of Comfort*,
    123–24
  of Vidal's minor works,
    141
  of *Washington, D. C.*, 71–
    72, 75
  of *Williwaw*, 34–37
  of *In a Yellow Wood*,
    120–21

Dark Green, Bright Red, 5,
    126–28
Day of the Locust, The
    (West), 94
death, 129, 130, 136
Death Before Bedtime, 5,
    136
Death in the Fifth Position,
    5, 136
Death Likes It Hot, 5, 136
"Death of Billy the Kid,
    The" (television script),
    6
"Death of Mishima, The,"
    110
Democracy (Adams), 91
Democritus, 59, 60
de Sapio, Carmine, 20
detective novels, 136–37
Didion, Joan, 30
Douglas, Melvyn, 6

Drug Enforcement Administration, 26
Dunne, Irene, 97
Dürrenmatt, Friedrich, 6, 138

Earhart, Amelia, 29, 30
Edgewater (mansion), 5
Edwards, Jonathan, 81
1876, 45, 67, 85–93
    American manners in, 87
    corruption in, 86, 88–89
    critique of, 91–93
    facades in, 89–90
    historical concepts in, 90–91
    New York setting in, 86–87, 90
    presidential campaign of, 85–86
    similarities to present-day figures in, 88
    theatrical allusions in, 89–90
Eisenhower, Dwight D., 140
"Erlinda and Mr. Coffin," 134–35
Esquire (periodical), 7
essays by Vidal, 110–17
    exposés among, 112
    humor and satire in, 113–15
    literary criticism in, 112–13
    power as a theme of, 111–12
    subjects of, 110–11
Evening with Richard Nixon and . . ., An, 7, 140

Everything You Always Wanted to Know about Sex (Reuben), 113
Eythe, William, 104

Faulkner, William, 6
Fear of Flying (Jong), 26
feminism, 95, 100
film scenarios of Vidal, 6
Ford, Gerald, 88
Francis, Kay, 97
"French Letters: Theories of the New Novel," 112
Frost, Robert, 119

Garbo, Greta, 104
Garland, Judy, 104
Gibbon, Edward, 10
Gide, André, 5, 20, 44
Gore, Nina (mother), 2, 3
Gore, Thomas Pryor, U. S. senator from Oklahoma, 1–3, 6, 111
Gore Vidal's Caligula (screenplay), 9
Grant, Julia Dent, 115–16
Grant, Ulysses, 86, 88, 110, 112
Graves, Robert, 58
Greene, Graham, 127

"Hacks of Academe, The," 113
Hall, Oakey, 86
Hamilton, Alexander, 76
Hancock, John, 76
Harlow, Jean, 96
Hawthorne, Nathaniel, 87
Hayes, Rutherford B., 86, 88
Hell's Angels (film), 96

Hemingway, Ernest, 10, 32, 35, 37, 39, 124, 131

Herodotus, 58, 62

historical novels
  of America's centennial, 85–93
  of ancient Persia, 58–66
  of early America, 75–85
  of early Christianity, 45–58
  on medieval Europe, 124–26
  of post-war America, 67–75

History (Herodotus), 62

Hitler, Adolf, 69

Homage to Daniel Shays: Collected Essays 1952–1972 (anthology), 110

homosexuality, 4, 5, 101, 107
  in *The City and the Pillar*, 37–44
  in *The Judgment of Paris*, 14, 16
  the Kinsey Report and, 40
  in "Pages from an Abandoned Journal," 135
  stigmatizing of, 37–38, 41
  in *Washington, D. C.*, 73–74
  in *In a Yellow Wood*, 119

Howe, Julia Ward, 87

humor, 15, 49, 51, 64, 139–40
  in *Washington, D. C.*, 71–72
  in *Myra Breckinridge*, 96–97
  in *Myron*, 102

  in Vidal's essays, 113–15

Hutton, Betty, 98

I Accuse (screenplay), 6

I Ching, 64

I, Claudius (Graves), 58

Ides of March, The (Wilder), 58

In a Yellow Wood, 4, 5, 118–21

In Our Time (Hemingway), 39

International Telephone and Telegraph, 111

IRS (Internal Revenue Service), 26

Irving, Washington, 80

Isherwood, Christopher, 5

Is Paris Burning? (film scenario), Vidal as contributor to, 6

Jackson, Andrew, 81

James, Henry, 6, 10, 88, 101, 108

Jealousy (Robbe-Grillet), 99

Jefferson, Thomas, 76, 78, 83

Jewett, Helen, 83

Johnson, Lyndon B., 111, 115

Jong, Erica, 26

Judgment of Paris, The, 5, 8, 11–17
  characterization in, 12, 13
  critique of, 13–14, 17
  myth in, 12

Julian, 8, 45–58
  Christian sects in, 48
  critique of, 49–51, 58

historicity of, 48
philosophy in, 53–54
religious conflicts in, 47,
    48, 52, 54–56
sections of, 47
sibling relationships in,
    56–57
Julian the Apostate, works
    of, 49
Jumel, Madame. *See* Bowen, Eliza

Kalki, 8, 24–31, 45
apocalyptic aspects of,
    24–25, 28
contemporary aspects of,
    26
critique of, 26–31
genocide in, 25, 27, 28
nihilism in, 28
religious cult of, 24
satire and humor in,
    26–27
villainy in, 25
Kennedy, John F., 140
Kerouac, Jack, 20
Kinsey Report, the, 40

"Ladies in the Library,
    The," 135–36
Lafayette, Marquis de, 76,
    82
Lawrence, D. H., 20
lesbianism, 95
liberalism, 112, 139–40
Lincoln, Abraham, 112
Lombard, Carole, 97
Look Homeward, Angel
    (Wolfe), 39
Lovejoy, Frank, 6

McAllister, Ward, 90
Macauley, Lord Thomas, 10
McCallister, Lon, 104
McCarthy, Eugene, Senator, 67
McCarthy, Joseph, Senator,
    69, 139
McCullers, Carson, 115
Mafia, the, 112
*Magic and Myth of the
    Movies* (Tyler), 98
Mailer, Norman, 101, 108
Mann, Thomas, 44
Manson, Charles, 115
Marcus Aurelius, 53, 54
Matters of Fact and of Fiction (anthology), 110
Merrywood, the Auchincloss estate, 72
Messiah, 5, 8, 45–46, 129–32
MGM   (Metro-Goldwyn-Mayer), 101, 102, 104
"Moment of Green Laurel,
    A," 3, 133–34
Montez, Maria, 101–2, 104
Moon, Sun Myung, 26
Moses, Robert, 111, 116
Myra Breckinridge, 8, 17,
    45, 94–100
androgynous aspects of,
    97
as camp literature, 96–98
conceit in, 96–97
critique of, 94, 100, 108–09
feminism in, 95, 100
rape in, 95, 99–100
sex change in, 94–95
transsexual conflicts of,
    97–98

Myron, 8, 45, 94, 100–09
  critique of, 102, 106
  film activities in, 100–02,
    104
  male sterilization in, 101,
    105
  priggishness of hero in,
    106, 108
  quality of humor in, 102
  real film stars in, 102, 104
  time-space concepts in,
    100, 103
  transsexual conflicts in,
    100–101, 105–06

Nabokov, Vladimir, 116
Napoleon, 79–80, 88
narcotics, 112
narration techniques, 132–
  33
Newman, Paul, 7
New Statesman (periodical),
  7
New York Review of Books
  (periodical), 7
New York Times, The (newspaper), 4, 111, 114
nicknames, 116
Night of the Generals, The
  (film scenario), Vidal as
  contributor to, 6
Nin, Anaïs, 3, 19
Nixon, Patricia, 111
Nixon, Richard M., 102,
  108, 111, 113, 139, 140
"Novelists and Critics of the
  1940's," 110

obscenity, 102
Omnibus (television program), 6

Onassis, Jacqueline, 19
On the March to the Sea,
  138

"Pages from an Abandoned
  Journal," 132, 134
Peckinpah, Sam, 108
*Personal Memoirs of Julia
  Dent Grant, The*
  (Grant), 115–16
Philadelphia Centennial
  Exposition, 86
Pilgrim's Progress (Bun-
  yan), 80
plays of Vidal, 6–7, 137–41
Poe, Edgar Allan, 73
"Police Brutality," 112
"Pornography," 110
power brokers, 111
Proust, Marcel, 20, 44
Pynchon, Thomas, 113

Radziwill, Lee, 19
rape, 39, 73, 95, 99, 105
*Reflections Upon a Sinking
  Ship* (anthology), 110
religion, 24, 33
  in *Creation*, 60, 62–65
  in *Julian*, 47, 48, 51–52,
    54
  in *Messiah*, 129–31
Renault, Mary, 61
Reuben, David, 113
Richard Coeur de Lion,
  124–25
Rimbaud, Arthur, 122
Ritchard, Cyril, 6
"Road Not Taken, The"
  (Frost), 119
Robbe-Grillet, Alain, 97
"Robin, The," 133

Rocking the Boat (anthology), 110
roman à clef, 19, 22, 32, 73, 122–23
Romulus, 6, 138–39
Roosevelt, Eleanor, 7, 20
Roosevelt, Franklin D., 2, 67

Sainte-Exupéry, Antoine de, 29
Santayana, George, 5
Scapegoat, The (film scenario), 6
Schuyler, Charlie, 76, 77, 80, 81–93
Search for the King, A, 5, 124–26
Season of Comfort, The, 5, 121–24
Serling, Rod, 6
"Sex and the Law," 110
Sex, Death and Money (anthology), 110
sexual concepts and activities, 12, 14, 16, 18, 20, 23
    in *The City and the Pillar*, 41–42
    heterosexuality and, 16, 39
    homosexuals and (*see* homosexuality)
    in *In a Yellow Wood*, 119
    in *Julian*, 56–57
    in *Kalki*, 23, 29
    in *Myra Breckinridge*, 95–97, 99–100
    in *Myron*, 104–06
    in *A Search for the King*, 125–26
    in *Washington, D. C.*, 73
Shakespeare, William, 91, 144
short stories of Vidal, 132–36
Simon, John, 115
60 Minutes (television show), 26
Solzhenitsyn, Alexander, 116
"Some Memories of the Glorious Bird," 114
Sontag, Susan, 114
Sothern, Ann, 97
Steers, Nina Auchincloss (sister), 19
Sterne, Laurence, 10
Stevens, Mrs. Paran, 90
Studio One (television program), 6
Subterraneans, The (Kerouac), 20
Suddenly, Last Summer (screenplay), 6
suicide, 15, 21–22, 29, 68
Sunday Showcase (television program), 6
Sun Myung Moon, 26
Suspense (television program), 6

television plays of Vidal, 5, 6
Thaxter, Phyllis, 97
Theodoret, 48
Thirsty Evil, A (anthology), 132
"Three Stratagems," 132–33

Tilden, Samuel J., 85, 86, 88, 90
time-space concepts, 100, 103
"Top Ten Best Sellers, The," 113
Townsend, Mrs., 80
transsexualism, 94–95, 97–98, 100–101, 105–06
Truman, Harry S, 137
Turner, Lana, 104
Turn of the Screw, The (James), television adaptation by Vidal, 6
Twain, Mark, 39, 87, 88
twin novels, 45
Two Sisters, 8, 17–24
  anecdotes in, 21
  dividedness in, 23
  as a *roman à clef*, 19, 22
  subtitles of, 17
"Two Sisters of Ephesus." See *Two Sisters*
Tyler, Parker, 98

"Une Saison en Enfer" (Rimbaud), 122

Van Buren, Martin, 76, 83
Vidal, Eugene Luther (father), 2
Vidal, Gore
  American ancestors of, 1
  arthritis of, 4
  birthplace of, 2
  the Bouvier sisters and, 19
  and William F. Buckley, Jr., 7
  change of name by, 3
  early writing career of, 4
  family tree of, 1, 2
  father of, 2
  as film writer, 6, 8
  foreign travels of, 8
  Senator Gore and, 1–3, 6
  Italian residence of, 8
  military service of, 4
  mother of, 2, 3
  as playwright, 6–7
  political activities of, 3, 7, 67
  political tracts of, 7
  public faces of, 1, 9
  schooling of, 2, 3
  sister of, 19
  as television writer, 5–6
Vidal's prose, observations on, 10–11, 30, 32, 37, 45, 142–44
  in *Burr*, 79, 82
  in *Creation*, 65–66
  in essays, 110–17
  in *Julian*, 50–51
  in *Messiah*, 131
  mock pomposity of, 115–16
  in *Myron*, 106–07
  in *The Seasons of Comfort*, 123–24
virility, 10, 106, 108
Visit to a Small Planet (stage play), 6, 140–41
Visit to a Small Planet (television play), 6, 137
voices, literary, 10

Washington, D. C., 8, 67–75
  critique of, 71–72, 75
  Freudian aspects of, 70
  historicity of, 70

homosexuality in, 73–74
humorous scenes from, 71–72
melodrama in, 70–71, 73–74
political aspects of, 68–69, 72
senatorial power in, 69
suicide in, 68, 71
Washington, George, 76, 78, 83, 140
Washington, Martha, 80
Weekend, 139–40
West, Nathaniel, 94
"West Point," 112
West Point, New York, 2
"What Robert Moses Did to New York City," 112
Wilde, Oscar, 71
Wilder, Thornton, 58

Williams, Tennessee, 5, 114
Williwaw, 4, 32–37
actors in, 35–37
author's restraint in, 37
characters of, 33, 35–36
critique of, 34–37
dialogue of, 35
as a *roman à clef,* 32
storm symbolism of, 33–34
Winesburg, Ohio (Anderson), 39
Wolfe, Thomas, 39
Wolfe, Tom, 88
Woodward, Joanne, 7, 104
Wouk, Herman, 114

"Zenner Trophy, The," 134
Zoroaster, 58–60, 63, 66

In the same series (*continued from page ii*)

FRANZ KAFKA   *Franz Baumer*
KEN KESEY   *Barry H. Leeds*
RING LARDNER   *Elizabeth Evans*
D. H. LAWRENCE   *George J. Becker*
C. S. LEWIS   *Margaret Patterson Hannay*
SINCLAIR LEWIS   *James Lundquist*
ROBERT LOWELL   *Burton Raffel*
GEORG LUKÁCS   *Ehrhard Bahr and Ruth Goldschmidt Kunzer*
NORMAN MAILER   *Philip H. Bufithis*
BERNARD MALAMUD   *Sheldon J. Hershinow*
ANDRÉ MALRAUX   *James Robert Hewitt*
THOMAS MANN   *Arnold Bauer*
MARY MCCARTHY   *Willene Schaefer Hardy*
CARSON MCCULLERS   *Richard M. Cook*
MARIANNE MOORE   *Elizabeth Phillips*
ALBERTO MORAVIA   *Jane E. Cottrell*
VLADIMIR NABOKOV   *Donald E. Morton*
ANAÏS NIN   *Bettina L. Knapp*
JOYCE CAROL OATES   *Ellen G. Friedman*
FLANNERY O'CONNOR   *Dorothy Tuck McFarland*
EUGENE O'NEILL   *Horst Frenz*
JOSÉ ORTEGA Y GASSET   *Franz Niedermayer*
GEORGE ORWELL   *Robert Kalechofsky*
KATHERINE ANNE PORTER   *John Edward Hardy*
EZRA POUND   *Jeannette Lander*
MARCEL PROUST   *James Robert Hewitt*
RAINER MARIA RILKE   *Arnold Bauer*
PHILIP ROTH   *Judith Jones and Guinevera Nance*
J. D. SALINGER   *James Lundquist*
UPTON SINCLAIR   *Jon Yoder*
ISAAC BASHEVIS SINGER   *Irving Malin*
LINCOLN STEFFENS   *Robert Stinson*
JOHN STEINBECK   *Paul McCarthy*
TOM STOPPARD   *Felicia Hardison Londré*
J. R. R. TOLKIEN   *Katharyn F. Crabbe*
LIONEL TRILLING   *Edward Joseph Shoben, Jr.*
JOHN UPDIKE   *Suzanne Henning Uphaus*
GORE VIDAL   *Robert F. Kiernan*
KURT VONNEGUT   *James Lundquist*
PETER WEISS   *Otto F. Best*
EUDORA WELTY   *Elizabeth Evans*
EDITH WHARTON   *Richard H. Lawson*
ELIE WIESEL   *Ted L. Estess*
OSCAR WILDE   *Robert Keith Miller*
THORNTON WILDER   *Hermann Stresau*
VIRGINIA WOOLF   *Manly Johnson*
RICHARD WRIGHT   *David Bakish*
EMILE ZOLA   *Bettina L. Knapp*
CARL ZUCKMAYER   *Arnold Bauer*